La Massane
Les Joncades Basses
13210 St-Remy-de-Provence

ISBN : 978-2-84135-607-2
www.editions-equinoxe.com

English edition

Provence

Photographs by
Gérard Sioen

Text by
Serge Bec

Translation by
Andrey Clarke & Marie Digne

ÉQUINOXE

PROVENCE

Serge BEC

"The world is divided in two: the border is located somewhere around the Loire. To the south of this line are small dark people who eat food cooked in olive oil and they are gods! To the north are fairhaired people who eat food cooked in butter…"

It wasn't an established chef who came out with this statement but the Spanish philosopher, Miguel de Unamuno. For the sake of those who might not have recognised these dark-comlexioned gods who cook with olive oil, let it be known that they are the people of Provence.

Unamuno exaggerates a little. The people of Provence are not gods even if everyone knows that Provence is blessed by them. But don't let's be mean in the denomination, let's simply allow one down-grading: they are demi-gods and let's have done with it!

What are we to say nowadays about this strange population of demi-gods whose art of living which is both profound and sensual is demonstrated through what we usually call, rather dismissively "good nosh". We might observe that to a certain extent they have forgotten this art of living, even if they continue the great Phoenician tradition of using olive oil. Their cooking, the foundation of civilisation, tends more and more to be swallowed up by commercially-produced frozen meals. We might willingly forgive them for having forgotten that Mistral was the winner of the Nobel Prize for Literature but not for forgetting the omelette aux truffes, les pommes d'amour persillées, la côtelette d'agneau de pays, la chouille de porc, la daube avignonnaise ou camarguaise, la brochette de petits oiseaux, la morue aux poireaux, les gratins d'aubergines et de courgettes, le fromage de chèvre, all washed down with local wine, Côtes-du-Rhône, du Ventoux, du Luberon, du Var, etc. For isn't a fact that you first learn to love a region through its food, in the same way that you learn to stay faithful to a wife?

Personally, I discovered Provence by lifting the lid of a stew or casserole which was simmering on the old stove belonging to my grandmother and by breathing in the aroma of the kebab of thrushes which was browning nicely in the large fireplace.

There is worse! I immediately recognised this Provence, my Provence on opening my innocent eyes to the world. And my first hesitant utterances were in the Provencal dialect. Without being aware, of course, that this my native land bore such a fine name and that the sounds heard by my young ears constituted myoriginal language, perhaps one of the most original of all languages and, in any case, one of the most beautiful.

There we have it: taste, smell, and hearing. As for sight, the first I had of Provence was the sight of a mountain – the Luberon and an unimportant little river – the Calavon. Two three-syllable names, one more rough because of the 'r' sound, the other more flowing thanks to a combination of the 'l' and the 'v' and the vowels, which have always seemed to me to contain the souls of those most ancient and mixed races, the Ligures, the first known inhabitants of the region and of the Greeks and Romans who came, saw and conquered, not to mention all the other Celts, Goths, Burgundians, Franks, Normans and Saracens (please ignore the lack of chronological order) who carried me away, in my youthful ignorance, to wild and brilliant Elysian fields.

In former times – I mean when I was a child – we never, or very rarely, called the Luberon by this name – the Luberon, visited today by all the northern intelligentsia who rob it of its extra-virgin cold pressed olive oil and seem to suck it in the mouth like a pot of lavender honey; we preferred to say *la colo* – the hill. As for the Calavon, we were on even more familiar terms, we abbreviated it to "Cala" and the Cala was this phenomenon which flows down from Banon (the village renowned for its goat's cheeses, served with a pinch of pepper and a drop of vinegar and wrapped in twelve sweet chestnut leaves. All the same, beware of dying of indigestion as happened, or so they say, to the emperor Antonin-the-Pious, born in 86 A. D...) and which then hits the barrier of the Luberon at the far edge of two "departements" of the Alpes de Haute-Provence and of the Vaucluse, after encountering the Gorges d'Oppedette (the secondlot after the Gorges du Verdon) and where, as the Luberon, it tries to dip its feet when there is some water. Often there is none. But when there is there is too much. Provence is always excessive, whether it rains, whether it is windy or whether the sun beats down. This is a fact which Mme de Sévigné well and truly grasped. In one of her many letters to her daughter Mme de Grignan, she wrote:

"How you do things to excess in Provence! Everything is extreme, your heat, your calm, your winds, your unseasonal rain, your autumnal thunderstorms: there is nothing mild or temperate. Your rivers break their banks, your fields are flooded and spoiled, your Durance always seems possessed by the devil."

Still during my childhood, the Cala was clear upstream of Apt, and reddish in colour downstream, because it would pick up the waters of the Doa, an unassuming large stream which collects all the modest little streams full of ochre from the Provencal Colorado which had not yet been given this title and which had not yet attracted the wondering gaze of the unfurling waves of hikers and the makers of advertising films. For the very good reason that this extraordinary location which kept recreating itself each day, was the permanent workplace of the men who produced ochre.

At Apt itself, the world capital of candied fruit, the capital of the Luberon and of Sainte-Anne, the Cala became the natural receptacle of effluents from the dozens of candied fruit factories set up in Caesar's ancient city, Apta Julia. On summer evenings on cafe terraces, the smell of rotten eggs (hydrogen sulphide) was certainly unbearable, but as it was not yet known that it was quite simply a case of pollution, the local sense of smell got used to it good-naturedly.

So the Cala was the first piece of the jigsaw to initiate me into the excesses of Provence, because of its smells, but especially because of its sudden downpours, when the spring or autumn sky poured more than 10 mm of water in an hour on Banon (an event which would mean that it could rain, in the region above the Loire, for more than a month). It was the first to make me feel the moods of nature in Provence and the stirrings of the flesh when it bestowed on my innocent gaze the unforgettable vision of a naked woman – a daughter of Provence of course – bathing in its troubled waters, whilst a few steps away I was deploying all my ingenuity with a length of string and a hook to lure a barbel out of the mud. My feelings were as troubled as the waters after this experience...

The emotions of the moment were prolonged in a sort of waking dream which had me flying over the creased and rumpled draperies of the young oaks of this androgynous beast, in deep repose, as if sated after making love since the dawn of time, and then had me alight on the vast replica of the two breasts I had seen on the water, a replica which was none other than the enormous breast – like crests of the Luberon, grazed by the flocks of a few Virgilian shepherds and watched by the orange eye of the Circaetus searching for its daily serpent.

My Provence had already taken on the form of a goddess and was offering her enticements to me.

And I truly think that it was from those very moments that there emerged from the confusion in which it was embroiled my great love for this land.

Then came the myth. I entered bodily into it and blew on the trumpet of renown to salute its glory: every mountain had to be magical or mystical, every walled town was of necessity Greek - Gallic - Roman in origin, every monument had to be Roman and its whole history of legendary proportions. To sum up, Provence spread over my adolescent bed with its voluptuously mythical indecency, with its indelible marks of the gods, indeed of God Himself.

It was a blind and therefore passionate love. Later, a stupid question called me to order: how should we love the object of our desire? By taking everything at its face value? By adoring without consideration? Or by searching for a further truth, with the risk of destroying the object of adoration?

So I lifted (with care and delicacy) the veil of certain acquired advantages. They seemed like the beauty emerging from the well: quite naked. And, as a result, stripped of their mystification. I was saddened by that. Notably, for example, when I had to bow to the evidence that Daudet's mill depicted in the postcards of Fontvieille was not his. For the moment my ancestors returned to their tombs. I reassured myself that mystification – if it had really existed – should be excused because, after all, it couldn't be imputed to the co-author of *Letters from my mill* (the other author being Paul Arène) but must be imputed to the readers, who, urged on subconsciously by the strange force of Provencal mythology, have peddled the cultural lie for the tourists, a lie for which Daudet left no pretext in his preface, apart from the imaginary choice of place names and characters (but these so intelligently derived from the Provencal l'*eime*).

"Gaspard Mitifio, manager of 'les Cigalières' and residing there with his wife Vivette Cornille, appeared before Maître Honorat Grapazi, notary at the Residence de Pampérigouste and sold to Alphonse Daudet, poet, residing in Paris, a windmill situated in the Rhone valley in the heart of Provence, on a wooded hill-side of pines and holm oaks; the aforementioned mill havng been abandoned for over 20 years and no longer in a fit state to be used as a mill, as is evident from the wild vines, mosses, rosemary bushes and other parisitic vegetation climbing over it right up to the sails. This notwithstanding, in the state it is in, with the great wheel broken and grass growing through the bricks, Alphonse Daudet declares the aforesaid mill to be to his liking, suited to writing poetry, and thus accepts it..."

The poetry-writing took over from the restoration works. The myth which has been damaged in my young head was saved in extremis by the fair-haired tourist desperate for southern exoticism. Well isn't that the essential thing? Isn't it more important, in this life of restraint bestowed upon us, that the poet should decorate illusion with reality's finery, especially when this poet comes from Provence? The cells of Edmond Dantes' Abbe Faria could never have existed, of course, except in the imagination of Alexandre Dumas. But it is so much the better for our individual imagination if we can see with our own eyes, in the Château d'If, the hole made in the wall through which Dantes was able to take the place of the Abbe's remains and escape from the maritime fortress. Didn't Pagnol do the same when he placed his César, Marius and Fanny against the background of the Vieux-Port? And Mistral, too, so that his traditional Provence of the middle of the 19th century should thus succeed in surviving beyond the industrial revolution, the nuclear age and the era of information technology? And Arène with his imaginary golden goat which guards a fabulous treasure hoard somewhere in Provence.

"A few hundred years ago, on the slopes of the Encourdoules Pass there could be seen on calm nights, grazing on mountain mosses or standing on the summit of a steep rock, a she-goat whose fleece had such a tawny hue that it could have been described as gold."

It only appeared at sunset. People do believe in it and pursue it. If only you knew how this beast born of the poetic imagination made me join the chase as well! I searched for it in Orange, at the bottom of a well on the hill of Saint-Eutrope, and it had taken refuge in an abandonned chapel in the Ventoux! I thought that I would be able to stroke it in Cabriès, near to Grasse. It showed the tip of its horns in Frejus or at Roquebrune or at Saignon or at Suze la Rousse in the Drôme! One of Nostradamus' quatrains declares that it is to be found in the ruins at Saint-Remy:

Beneath the ancient ruins, vestal edifices
Not far from a ruined acqueduct
Of sun and moon are the gleaming metals
The flaming light, Traian of burnished gold.

Of course, Traian is the golden male goat, but to get from the male of the species to the female there is only the accident of birth. So I hurried to the ancient ruins and it was in those of the Abbey of Montmajour that there were tales of the goat's whereabouts. From Montmajour I crossed to Fontvieille. Yvan Audouard had believed that he had caught sight of it through the flight holes of his pigeon loft. Exhausted, I found myself dreaming that sometimes the goat basked in the sun on a limestone peak in the sunlight of les Baux. I climbed les Baux. In vain. However I heard the faraway echo of the love song of Vincent to Mireille:

T'ame que se disien ti labro:
Vole la Cabro d'or, la cabro
Que degun de mortau ni la pais ni la mous
Que sout lou ro de Baus-Maniero,
Lipo la moufo roucassiero,

O me perdrieu dins la peiriero,
O me veiries tourna la cabro dóu peu rous!

(I love you to the point that if you were to say - I want the Golden goat, the goat - Which no mortal puts out to pasture or milks - Which, beneath the rock of Baus-Maniere - Grazes on wild moss - Either I would lose my life in the stone quarries - Or I would bring you the goat with the auburn fleece.)

Finally it was in the white hills of Estaque, in the little village of Rove on the western outskirts of Marseille, famous for its goat's milk *brousse* (cheese) that I flushed her out. I'm sure that it's her, the goat of Rove, which gave birth to the myth of the *Golden Goat*. Isn't she more beautiful, more fantastical, more strange than her cousins and her lyre-shaped horns and tawny coat shine with reflections of gold in the rays of the setting sun. She can survive in the poorest, most isolated places, where, in fact, legend places her. And then, doesn't the species date back to the very dawn of time? Native of Mesopotamia the Rove goat was disembarked from the long ships (vessels propelled by sail and oars) along with the olive branch of peace and the vine of pleasure when the Phoenicians berthed at Lacydon. It was this species of goat which was roasted for the wedding of Nannus, king of the Ligurian tribe of the Ségobriges, and the beautiful Gyptis whose name is not without links with the Gypsies of the Camargue region whose patron saint is Sara. We must remember that this ceremony took place in 600 B.C. to found Massalia.

In this way, myth in Provence is the stumbling block of poetry, nothing can be resolved.

And even Giono, whom we can hardly accuse of complicity in what I have just described, – has he done anything which does not substantiate the Provencal mythology, superimposed on reality, reinvented at each step forward, at each penstroke, at each of his inventions. How can we visit Manosque without visiting Giono, his gateway of Aubette *"through which dawn enters the town"*, or the fountain of the Observantines, or the "little deserted squares where, from the moment of my arrival, at the height of the summer sun, Œdipus has his eyes put out…", or even his symbolic Mont d'Or, *"this fine round breast is a hill… the plain comes to milk its springs then goes away, fecund with trees and corn."* Indeed, Giono who claimed: *"There is no Provence. Whoever loves it loves the world or loves nothing." "Whoever loves it"*. Loves what? Well, Jean, your Provence, of course!

Let's return to my Provence of the *pedas* (literally the Provence which existed at the time of my entry into this world). Between the Luberon, Calavon and the Monts de Vaucluse, it was steeped in exceptional diversity of geology, landscape, vegetation, flora and fauna, monuments and individuals. The Apt region is a concise synthesis of the geoculture of Provence and – I was going to add *of the world* if I had not heard in advance the mocking voices whispering: "He's from Provence, so he must be exaggerating!" This synthesis has always been polarised towards the high ground. At least, as far as I'm concerned. I mean both towards the Alps of Haute-Provence – Oh, I feel a nostalgia for the "Basses-Alpes"! – and towards the high plateaus which are not really the mountains in the true sense of the word. But not towards the low ground, that is following the meanders of the Rhone through the plains of Basse-Provence. Except for a diversion however in the direction of the Mediterranean, after which I have always longed with an unquenchable thirst.

"It's your roots which always tug at you, my lad!" my grandmother always used to say. And these strange roots, which go in the opposite direction to normal roots, always draw me up to the high ground.

By the high ground I mean the sentimental landscape which, starting from its centre at Apt raises me physically and spiritually all over the Durance, between Luberon, Ventoux, Lure, up to Digne across the regions of Manosque and Forcalquier up to Sisteron across the Jabron valley. In this vast expanse stretch out the plateaus which are as one with the breath of the huge trees which push against the hymen of the heavens, which cry out in the abysses of the skies. I speak of these high plateaus which couple with infinity to create the constellations, where you feel lost in the infinity of light as in the brutal unexpectedness of a storm, but where you are always filled with the intuition of your own rebirth on the other side of a vast death.

I cannot evoke the extraordinary names of places without a tremor going up my spine, setting me all on edge and making my heart beat erratically: Col de l'Homme Mort, Pas de Redortier, Combe de Malcourt,

Mallefougasse, Silance, Ferrassières, Vaumale, les Cavaliers... Names which are to be found from the Plateau d'Albion to Contadour and all about Verdon, from the Plateau of Valensole to the Grand Plan de Canjuers.

I have travelled madly through these high landscapes, the background to Giono's imaginary sedentary manosquin. I have thrown myself like a lost soul into the fiery coals of this solitary Creation, into the timeless convulsions of this ancient tragedy.

Here, men and women have come from far away, perhaps from the dark silence of lightning flashes, perhaps they are lost voices in quest of living death, across the vicissitudes of time feeding on a sprig of thyme, on the *pebre d'ase* or on aspic, bending over the horizon of sky and rock, heads buzzing with the sound of the bees and the prickling sensation of the old legends, which mingle once more with the reality of each new day.

Here, men and women, fettered by iron solitude, stir up the passions of this ungrateful land, where they only exist with their internal cry, which, like a horn in the mouth of an unfathomable pothole, echoes in the ears of sombre light.

Here, men and women have overcome a thousand deaths at sunset in the villages and farms, representing, in the infinite sea of their sweat, a future of sun and storms.

In a state of delirium provoked by wind, sun and rock, you can with impunity address as familiars the enormous heroic trees which loom up out of the night of plants. Only the gods can hear you and record your monologues. That is fortunate, since, if the people of the fertile valleys and watery plains were to hear you, they would take you for the last of the lunatics.

In the petrified gestures of the fantastic, silent being, relentlessly pursuing a thirst for inner galaxies, you can reduce yourself to nothingness in the winds which sweep everything before them and which cause the infinite limits of the horizon to bang like a door, sending their echoes back and forth, sowing in the ploughed fields claims for great joy. Your eyes may wander through hardy grasses witnessing storms lighting up the vastness of the sky and also through the stronghold of many rocky furrows, in the reflection of the huge sphere of the setting sun.

You have to experience them directly, personally, these deserted landscapes of blue lavender, with their subtle, bitter perfume, like stony seraglios, where men and women, enjoying a temporary immortality, sing deep within themselves the song of transfixing death.

It is here that I dreamed about misletoe betrothals, tumultuous visionaries of the void which dazzled me like the fossilized spume of an upside-down sea.

These familiar or unfamiliar ghosts rise up from the land of the ancient Albici ligures and are there at your finger tips. Here is the mighty, faceless figure of the wife of François-Louis d'Agoult, the proud Chretienne d'Aguerre, Countess of Sault, whose incredible adventures with the Duke of Savoy in Aix-en-Provence ornamented the Wars of Religion. She was a powerful woman devoted to defending her ideals in the violent world of the second half of the XVIIth century in Provence and who dealt as an equal with the sovereigns of Europe. What haven't we ascribed to her: unscrupulous ambition, numerous love affairs, family crimes! Her great part in legend does not, however, stop her resembling the women of the region which she quickly made her own. In the County of Sault, nothing remains of the castle of the Agoult family except for four round towers striving to hold up their heads above the rest of the architectural entity, which is divided up into private dwellings for people living in the village. The lords of Sault, vassals of the Count of Forcalquier the most influential nobles of the XIIth century would build the surprising and mysterious "Rotunde de Simiane" with its twelve arches ending in a diagonal line around an enigmatic lantern.

It would seem that Raymond d'Agoult, a great patron of the Troubadours, not only in Provence but in the whole of the Langue d'Oc (Cadenet, Elias de Barjols, Peire Vidal praised him in their songs) is said to have constructed it for them to perform in. If this was the case, then the Rotunde has today rediscovered its vocation, across the centuries, since it is a prime venue for concerts.

Here are to be found the painters Eugène Martel du Revest-du-Bion, Ambrogiani who, thanks to his friendship with René Seyssaud, came to work at Aurel, then at Sault, his last resting place since 1985; Othon Coubine, the Czech from Simiane.

Here is Kléber Constantin, the bee-keeper, at Saint-Christol.

In 1966, René Char, living in the neighbouring L'Isle-sur-Sorgue, launched his manifesto against the setting up of the nuclear base, a manifesto illustrated by Picasso and called *Provence point Omega*:

"May those who are drilling into the noble earth's crust at Albion take account of this: we are fighting for a site where the snow is not only winter's wolf but the alder of the spring. The sun rises on our demanding blood and man is never a prisoner in his neighbour's house. In my eyes, this site is worth more than our daily bread, because it is irreplacable."

Each time I climb Albion, one vision obsesses me: that of the terrible and awesome black horse of legend carrying away from one of the limestone tombs where burn the fires of hell, Arnold, the son of the Lord of Saint-Christol.

The plateau of Albion and the plateau of Valensole are the authorised guardians of the lavender pictured on postcards, the typical image of Provence for all Northeners.

I was 18 and to make a little money during the holidays, two friends and I got a job on a farm on Mont Amaron, in the commune of Lagarde (where Lea, now sadly deceased, used to concoct her wonderfully aromatic jugged hare at her inn) the end of the plateau of Albion as it overhangs the Apt valley. At the end of July and beginning of August, we were up at 5 a.m. and, shattered, exhausted, after a ten-hour working day, we used to sleep in the straw. Far from the idyllic postcard images! We had to march on through the interminable sea of violet, through the arc of the sickles cutting the sweetsmelling stems as we circled round the plant, slicing through the void of terrible light which lends an air of tragedy to the least shadow it creates or destroys. Where others would be done for after an hour, the swarm of cutters only stops at nightfall. They resemble enormous locusts, descending from other lands with their huge blue and white wings, wildly devouring the waves of mauve flowers, which the bees suck and which send vipers to sleep. In particular, I recall one of the last workers to cut lavender by hand. This was Jouse, who came from Piémont at an early age and who continued to cut lavender at the age of 79, in order "not to lose his touch"! He was the one who refused to be photographed because he didn't want to have his identity stolen, in other words, his soul! Unfortunately for country traditions, for the beauty of the countryside and for the tourists, the lavender cutters with their rough cloth bags knotted across their shoulders like a modern-day car seat belt are hardly ever to be seen in the fields stretching to the horizon; they have been replaced by machines.

The Contadour is a stone's throw away, with its dry-stone walled sheep pens and its "fraches". How else can we view it other than through the eyes of Giono and his friends at the time of their Utopian, community adventure? Great expanses of waves which may be rounded or unfurling according to the state of the skies. A group of bushes which climb triumphantly, in Indian file, like hussars on the roof of the world towards the unknown or which, alternatively, return downtrodden, depending on the state of the skies which are constantly changing. This Provencal wilderness keeps a sharp eye out in its state of rocky expectation.

The Contadour is already the Lure. I can see myself one December in a freezing coach specially hired for the occasion, with boys and girls from Apt college, stopping at Saint-Etienne-les-Orgues to have a coffee, before starting the ascent to the Lure summits. We were about to learn to ski! A cousin from Viens, Paul Bouquet, had lent me his long, heavy pair of skis with straps that went all round my calves. The Lure awaited us! Since this first encounter, of all the mountains in Provence, it's the wild, secret, indefinable Lure which captivates me, which turns my head. On the Lure, I saw the fascinating shadows dancing around the old fire beneath *l'estello dòu Bouvie, le Grand Carri, les Tres Rei ou le Bastoun de Jan de Milan*. Were they the ghosts of witches who haunt the night? I tore them apart on the wild summit where they vanish at morning. Oh Lure! I can hear your savage breathing and the faint noise of the deer, wild boar and all the animals as their bodies brush against the trees, and I shout out, I announce the newness of the world and its eternity! 40 000 hectares without a living soul. Hillsides and clumps of pine, beeches, larches, wild strawberries and raspberries. An abbey, Saint-Donat's, an offshoot of Boscodon near to Embrun. And a mystery to tell. In the XVIIIth and XIXth centuries, the undulations of the Lure were the haunt of herbalists who came to harvest the marvellous plants which could cure anything and which supplied apothecaries throughout the kingdom. To the north at an altitude of 1 826 metres, the magnificent Jabron valley opens up like a scar across Sisteron. One of my friends hunts hare in this area, on the high hills of Saumane, between Lure, Contadour, Contras and Jabron, not far from the great "oppidum" of Chastelard-de-Lardiers. It often happens that his dogs raise the hares and do not come back. The next day he goes to get them back from the Jabron valley, between Noyer and Séderon where he calmly waits for them to return exhausted. Neither dogs nor man can get lost in these solitary places.

I hope that it will not displease my learned friends of the remarkable *Carnets du Ventoux* that I climbed the Giant of Provence not to emulate Petrarch, nor to observe the difference between its Mediterranean and alpine vegetation, nor to admire its flora first studied by Jean-Henri Fabre and to go into raptures over the rare oppositeleaved saxifrage which attracts the attention of any botanist arriving in July on the shores of Spitzberg, nor even to ski at Chalet Reynard or on Mont Serein, but to see the competitors in the Tour de France go by! Everyone has his little foibles!... Whether it's in the face of Louison Bobet radiating pain and joy, in Simpson's lifeless body or in the anxiety of Eric Caritoux, a native of this land, I could read as in an open book the power and fascination of this isolated pyramid 1909 metres in altitude. It is both light and crushing, like a Janus with two faces, the north face sheer, wild, lugubrious and the sunny south face pointing towards the sea with its smiling white stony aspect which the glare of the sun transforms into snow. It's this face which has imprinted itself on my memory. Ever present and ever elusive, the Ventoux is a mirage which all the writers have paid homage to, including René Char who describes it as the "mirror of eagles".

Allow me to call upon Marie Mauron to introduce it:

"Over the Comtat Venaissin and Provence, the Ventoux reigns incontestable and uncontested, our pagan god. What is better still is that the whole of the South of France can see it from all directions and from all directions it has a different aspect. It is the Ventoux long before the Virgin of la Garde, the Bonne Mère of Marseille, that the sailors watch from out at sea – and from right out at sea! – the first to signal a welcome and the last to disappear as a sign of farewell, or rather a "till we meet again"! From the Camargue and from Crau it seems like a lapis lazuli Fuji-Yama in good weather, a formidable aquamarine if a storm is brewing. From Avignon it is the blue giant which, at each forward step dominates the horizon and the road. It's from Bédoin, from Malaucène, from Carpentras, from Sault when it's really close up where you can look at it fondly, almost touch it with your hand that the Ventoux plays at hide and seek, at changing its fantastic shape according to the whim of the smallest ridge, the tiniest copse of truffle-bearing oaks or of pines, to reappear in a guise dictated by a certain indentation, to reveal itself in its entirety from the summit of a peak or from the sudden wide platform of a plateau!"

From the Sommet des Tempêtes, the whole Roman Provincia of earlier times is there, beneath your feet, with its natural boundaries – The Mediterranean, the Rhone, the Alps, forming an horizon with a central emblem, the point of the Ventoux which Mistral and Aubanel (among others) have glorified.

So many things to see, to show, so many landscapes, so many images to portray, stories to tell, names to quote! So mush history! So much hope to announce! What confusion too, what a mix, what chaos! From the summit of the Ventoux, perhaps you have to start from scratch and begin again to write a history of Creation, as did the extraordinary accursed writer from Althen-les-Paluds, André de Richaud! I shall be content to say that the Ventoux belongs, above all, to the Vaucluse.

The departement which in 1793 took the name of Vallis Clausa a legacy of the Romans, resembles a jigsaw puzzle in which every piece forged its own destiny: the Pontifical states of Avignon and the Comtat Venaissin, the Principality of Orange, the Comte of Sault and la Viguerie of Apt. This valley which seems to have been caught in the trap of the enormous cliff face, the source of the Fountain of Vaucluse, is nevertheless an open country. It is an area of contact between the Alps and the plain, between the South and the North, between Provence and Languedoc and, with its agricultural orientation, it has always been able to adapt, to model itself according to temporary demands or eternal situations and to create for itself an image of long friendship, where the countryman and the city dweller are fully integrated.

It is via the Rhone and its inalienable book of legends that access is gained. The legend of Bénézet, pastor of Vivarais at the beginning of the XIIth century, who was ordered by a heavenly voice to follow the river to Avignon and to build a bridge there. This he did with the help of a guardian angel and people have danced on this bridge (only half of it remains now) for a long period of time.

The Rhone only provides a border to the Vaucluse over a distance of about sixty kilometres. But that suffices to breathe into it a myth of modern times: the project of the Rhone-Rhine link, joining the Mediterranean with the North Sea. There is yet another myth, which took shape with the Donzère-Mondragon developments, activating the turbines of the huge hydro-electric power station (named André Blondel) at Bollène, the town where Pasteur discovered an important vaccine. Since the XIth century, the taming of the Rhone has exercised eminent minds. The Popes brought engineers from Italy. In the more recent past, the technicians from the Compagnie Nationale du Rhône and the Société du Canal de Provence have taken over the job. The Blondel works have enabled to set up nuclear installations at Tricastin: Pierrelate, Marcoule, Eurodif which all enrich uranium by gas diffusion.

Mistral has said that Pont-Saint-Esprit was *"la porto santo e courounello de la terro d'amour"* (the eminent, sanctified gate-way to the land of Love), thanks to this bridge between Languedoc, Auvergne and Vivarais on which the mistral wind and the Rhone seem to come together definitively. Pont-Saint-Esprit is better known for the terrible news item of 1951 about the "accursed bread" and for the two hundred or so distant relatives of Jacky Kennedy whose great-great-grandfather Michel Bouvier went to settle in Philadelphia in 1815, joining his friend Joseph Bonaparte in exile after his abdication from the throne of Spain.

However, spiritual and physical entry into the Vaucluse takes place through the magnificent Arc de Triomphe at Orange *la poumpouso*, the opulent. It owes its renown especially to the "Chorégies" created in 1869 by Anthony Réal and Félix Ripert, and to its huge amphitheatre, the "Théâtre Antique" with its great wall held in such awe by actors and divas, more than to the town's real hero, Guillaume le Taciturne, the last of the Princes of Orange, and not to forget the traditional Guillaume au Court-Nez (of the short nose). This glorious past has been carried all over the world: to South Africa, to Australia, to Canada and to the United States, where more than 60 towns revel in the name of Orange!

Orange is also the wine capital of the Côtes-du-Rhône. These wines could only be created in the secret of the rounded stones of the ancient bed of the Durance, on the hillsides of Châteauneuf-du-Pape whose history mingles with that of the Papacy in Provence. Clément V, the first Pope made the journey on his mule (which made the mule's kick famous), with ham, eggs, bread and a good flask of wine.

Félix Gras, the author of *Li Rouge dóu Miejour*, sang about it mischievously: to bring out a certain trait in the Pope's character: *"Dison qu'es un lapin - Lou Papo, lou Papo - Dison qu'es un lapin - Lou Papo Clement V!"* (let's say that he's a bit of a lad - the Pope Clement V!) But it was his successor Jean XXII who made the fortune of Châteauneuf when he built the castle, his summer residence, there and became the first winemaker. The prince of winemakers will always be the Baron Le Roy de Boiseaumarie who created the "Appellation d'origine contrôlée" and who is to Châteauneuf-du-Pape what The Marquis of Baroncelli-Javon is to the Camargue (his family is the owner of the Château des Fines Roches). If Châteauneuf-du-Pape is the uncontested jewel in the crown of the Côtes-du-Rhône, about sixty communes with a lesser grading – but not necessarily with lower alcohol proof – produce such famous wines as Gigondas, Cairanne, Sablet, Sainte-Cécile-les-Vignes, Vacqueyras the homeland of the celebrated troubadour Raimbaut. How better to describe these wines than leave it to Baron Le Roy:

"Here, sirs, take a bow please... gleaming in its cardinal red, warmed by the Provencal sun, aromatic with the scent of the garrigues, vibrant with the song of crickets, it has as its grand finale a firework display of the great wines of the Rhone hillsides."

At Vaison-la-Romaine, the ancient ruins take pride of place again. Here everyone is an archeologist since excavations from 1907 to 1926 allowed Canon Sautel to uncover the Gallo-Roman town dating from the first and second centuries and its exceptional amphitheatre, 96 metres in diameter. The restoration was completed by Jules Formiguié, the chief architect of Historic Monuments. André burrus, an industrialist from Alsace king of the Swiss tobacco industry, learned that a citizen of Vaison, Nero's preceptor, answered to the name of Afranius Burrus and thus decided to allow the town access to his personal fortune. As a result, veritable treasures came to light like the famous statue of Diadumenus, the masterpiece by Polycletus, a Greek sculptor of 4 B.C. (The original is in the British Museum). Unfortunately, since the terrible Ouvèze flood which only left the single arch (with an opening of 17,20 m by 9 m wide) of the Roman bridge standing, Vaison bears another title, that of the martyred town.

Further on the Enclave de Valréas, an outpost of the departement of Vaucluse detached in the Drome, makes the transition with the Baronies. Valréas draws pride from this exceptional situation. Jules Niel who was practically mayor of Valréas for life and President of the General Council of Vaucluse for many years, stated one day:

"Enclaves are not a commonplace. So when you have one to offer, you keep it for yourself and pamper it!"

On the other side of the Lez, Grignan and its castle make a big impression on Tricastin and the daughter of Mme de Sévigné who brought her there to cure her wasting disease. She married there in 1669 the local lord of the manor, the very ugly Comte Adhémar, lieutenant general of Provence.

Let's cross quickly into the Baronies to attend the traditional festival of the lime-blossom tea at Buis-les-Baronnies and to salute the olive, the little queen of Nyons. We shall taste a few while reading the letter which Giono wrote on February 24th 1964 to M. René Duchet, the President of the committee organising the Festival of the Olives:

"Yes, of course, I accept, and thank you for, your invitation to be honorary president of the Confrérie des Chevaliers de l'Olive. In as much as I am the owner of three hundred olive trees and see to the harvest personally with my wife, my secretary and my maid, and have the oil made under my own supervision in the oldest mill possible and that since the age of seventy, I have never used olive oil other than my own. Olive oil is the most important of all the foodstuffs I eat. I even take some with me when I go to Paris!"

However the Popes are the ones who have written the great history of the region in the XIVth century when a prestigious destiny awaited Avignon. A destiny which was played out almost unbeknown to the town, in the raging battles fought beneath the walls of the Vatican by the Colonna and the Orsini, the two rival families. If I may say so, that was all that was required for it to be the time of the Avignon Popes! The first was fetched from Bordeaux; the Archbishop of this town, Bertrand de Got was elected to the Holy See, after the Conclave of Pérouse, and took the title of Pope Clément V. After moving around for four years, he finally settled in Avignon in 1309. There was a very precise reason for this choice: the town belonged to the Comtes of Provence, the kings of Naples and vassals of the Holy See. Clément V would therefore have felt on friendly ground. His name will remain linked with the trial of the Order of Templars. He would die on the other side of the Rhone, at Roquemaure, in 1313, a town which would see Placide Capeau compose his *Minuit Chrétien* nine centuries later, which was set to music by Adam.

As for his successors, we shall have to look for them in Occitania. The first was Jean XXII, the son of a Cahors cobbler. He started the formidable task of building the Palace continued by his successors: Benoit XII, the son of a baker from the Pyrénées, Clément VI 'the Magnificent', the former guardian of the royal seals, who received the submissions of Queen Jeanne, the countess of Provence (the embodiment of another great myth in Provence), queen of Naples, of Sicily and of Jerusalem, who had come to justify the murder of her husband. Absolution cost her the town of Avignon; then came Innocent VI, the former master of the university of Toulouse, who had the imposing ramparts built around the town to protect it from the hordes of English mercenaries; Urbain V, former monk from the abbey of Saint-Victor de Marseille had a passion for botany; finally Grégoire XI who dreamesd of returning to Rome, which he did on September 13th 1376.

For all that the papal history of Avignon was not yet closed. The "antipopes"' continued to dispute the papal throne of Avignon. By turns, Clément V, Benoît XIII, Clément VIII, and Benoît XIV pronounced the excommunication of their Roman counterparts. Through the issuing of papal bulls, the latter did the same. It was the great schism which divided the Christian world. Finally Rome triumphed. It was the papal legates who occupied the Palace. Over a period of 350 years, 98 of them became heads of the administration in Avignon.

In fact, Avignon, the Eternal City on the banks of the Rhone, only had the privilege of replacing Rome for 70 years, the life-span of a single man. But seven Popes contributed to its glory with their Palace which people visit from all over the world. A Palace which welcomes into its Court of Honour the festival created by Jean Vilar, the pope of the theatre, who gave universal cultural fame to it.

At the foot of the Ventoux, the cultivated terraces which are called in these parts *restanques* or *bancaus* are the glory of the countryside. Here Georges Stéphane Giraud, the fine poet from Bédoin, depicting this region through the essence of its land glorified in all the multiplicity of its moods, writes:

"Raising our head, we find a countryside of warm breaths, with the arrogance of a mirror. Our ancient immortality looks at itself and listens to itself. Beyond all caution, we caress the gods".

Between the plains of the Ouvèze and Comtat, stretching over a dozen kilometres, the Dentelles de Montmirail, veritable festoons of saw teeth like immense ruined ramparts, sing an ode to joy, to which the Muscat de Beaumes-de-Venise is no stranger. Beaumes-de-Venise has never been the capital of the Doges, having as its only Grand Canal the little canal leading to a dip in the Venaissin, the Comtat which Vénasque gave his name to (or so it is said) and whose capital was Pernes-les-Fontaines before Carpentras, the Jewish town whose synagogue built in the XVIIIth century is one of the finest in all France and whose Inguimbertine library has more than 150 000 works, for the most part works of antiquity.

If you haven't been to Fontaine-de-Vaucluse at least once in your life then you don't deserve forgiveness! Petrarch, who settled there in 1337 until 1353, had time to write 88 odes to his mysterious Laura, perhaps the wife of Hugues de Sade. On September 8th 1533, Francois I traced with his hand, inscribed on Laura's false tomb, lines written by the Italian poet who had become Provencal. The Romantic poets always made a sentimental journey to Fontaine-de-Vaucluse. In his *Mémoires d'Outre-Tombe* Chateaubriand tells of his visit to these parts in 1802. The memory of Petrarch has not vanished into thin air and his semi-legendary love for Laura de Noves has even filtered down into local commerce.

The fountain – in its Provencal meaning of spring – is the most important of its kind in the world, when it is full, reaching an output of 185 000 litres per second. What is its mystery? Does it come from an underground river which collects the rain water from the immense Vaucluse plateau and maybe from elsewhere? Potholers and cavers of olden and modern times, Martel, Casteret, Cousteau and the recent use of sonar have not yet been able to explain the enigma. Whatever the explanation, the water, issuing like an animal in rut from its hole, allows the Sorgue (which also means 'spring' in the Provencal language) or, I ought to say, the sorgues, to give to the towns and countryside which they pass through a welcome freshness in summer and a calm serenity in general, as is the case in Isle-sur- Sorgue, from which René Char drew his inspiration.

Châteauneuf-de-Gadagne is a quiet little town on high ground between Isle-sur-Sorgue and Avignon. It's claim to fame has been inscribed in the stone of the little castle of Font-Ségugne since the name day of Sainte-Estelle on May 21st 1854 when the cultural destiny of Provence was drastically changed. Thanks to a few enthusiastic young men ready to move mountains to get their ideas accepted, seven mad poets (as you tend to be at the age of twenty) led by Frédéric Mistral. The others were Joseph Roumanille, Théodore Aubanel, Paul Giéra, Jean Brunet, Anselme Mathieu and Alphonse Tavan. They constituted the famous seven *primadie* who, on that day, founded that strange association which they called the Félibrige! This term was made up from the word "fe libre", which is found in the old song *L'oraison de Saint Anselme* where it is said that Jesus was in the temple with the seven Félibres or Doctors of Law. The following play on words interested them and even seemed a premonition: in Provencal, "fe libre" can mean at one and the same time "free faith" and "to act freely" and "to make books". They took on an ambitious programme: to restore the Provencal language, giving it an orthography which had been lost over the centuries when it was only spoken; to use it in literature, especially poetry, and to claim the right for it to be taught in schools. The "Félibrige", although a little restricted by successors who worship too much the myth of Mistral, nevertheless remains a movement with ideas and a plan of action which has no equal in Provence.

If I had really structured my initiatory tour of Provence, I should have gone down the Durance from Sisteron. All the more so because it is the Durance which allows everything. Far from being one of the three plagues of Provence, (as in the XVI century, along with the mistral and the parliament) it gave birth to civilisation, it gives man his daily bread and his joy, even if, from time to time, man has to suffer its rebellion, like any subservient being. From Sisteron up to its confluence with the Rhone at Avignon, it is omnipresent. It breaks its natural barriers at the "cluse de Sisteron", at the narrow gorges of Mirabeau, Mallemort, Orgon and Bonpas. It splits the mountain in two, cascading over its stones. At Manosque and South Luberon, it sprawls across the vast plains, marked out in squares by the orchards which it fertilises. It greets the "oppida ligures" which watch its cascades. It is alive; I prefer it to the Rhone, which can be likened almost to the Minotaur in that it brought to our towns the fair-and red-haired beer-swigging barbarians and the Aryans with their evil destiny; and, for this, I bear it a grudge. Fortunately, so says my friend, the Occitanian poet, Yves Rouquette, it redeems itself by creating the Camargue!

You cannot really talk about the Durance without describing the Serre-Ponçon dam between le Champsaur and les Monges, between Embrun and Gap, with its lake as big as the one at Annecy. This construction, which rises 120 metres above the river bed, 650 metres thick and 100 wide, retains 1200 cubic metres of water for the EDF (Electricité de France) and was put into action in 1959. It is the key to the river management and its new character: it regulates the flow and allows a measured supply of water into the irrigation channels of the Vaucluse and the Bouches-du-Rhône. Should we be for or against the harnessing of the *Living Water* (the title of the first feature film by Jean Giono whose subject was the construction of the infamous dam, Giono being against the subjugation of the Durance.)? I believe that there should be a permanent balance between man and nature, each at the service of the other.

So it is at Sisteron that the Durance has to use its force to bring down the rock between the "titanesque gendarme's cap" of La Baume and the citadel which Henri III prided himself in saying was the strongest in his kingdom. François I crossed the pass three times; coming back from Marignan, before the Battle of Pavie and in 1537, but I do not remember on which occasion that time.

For 400 years, 82 prelates (I haven't counted them but rely on earlier statistics) have held the Archbishopric of this town. The cathedral houses the tomb of one of them, Monseigneur de Glandevès-Cuges. It was in the convent of the Cordeliers that Raimond Bérenger IV, count of Provence in the XII century, surrounded by his court, wrote his will, in which he left his lands to his younger daughter Béatrix whom we shall rediscover at Forcalquier in the company of Pierre Magnan who reveals to us the secrets of old Sisteron.

From here The Eagle, returning from Saint-Helena really took off. If Sisteron had allowed him to pass he would have said: *"I am in Paris!"* He slept at the Auberge du Bras d'Or, run by the grandfather of a famous native of Sisteron, namely Paul Arène. It isn't the golden goat but an arm of gold all the same! Here the first cricket sang from time immemorial, the self-same one heard by Jean des Figues, when lying in the shade of a donkey's shadow, he became a poet!

So, here, one region ends – the Dauphine – and another begins, Provence. Here, the olive and the cypress decide to link their destinies once and for all. It is from Sisteron, *clau de Provenco* as Mistral would say, that, following the course of the Durance, at each milestone, you die of longings as old as the solar solitude of the world. And when I experience deep inside a great need of the Durance, I go up to Ganagòbi (which is pronounced quite differently in the Provencal language.) It is a name which has always beckoned me. I say it out loud, just for the pleasure of making the sounds, butting up against the two "g" whilst rolling the vowels around the mouth like the pebbles of the Durance, for no other reason than to suck the sap from the great tree of time.

Ganagòbi is a synthesis of the great mystical, luminous force of Provence, where pagan faith and God's grace freely intermingle. It contains them, it brings them together and exalts them. On each of my adventures in Ganagòbi, I see, as if it were a symbol, the silhouette of the little monk whom I had followed the first time on the high pathways. He goes on his way, in deep silence, urged on by the invisible breath of God along the Allée des Moines, beneath the green and black vault of the holm oaks which is pierced by glimmers of the sky, in which it is set like a jewel. This Allée was painted by Monticelli, who lived here for a time during his childhood, raised by his nurse at the farm adjacent to the monastery. It links the priory to the far end of the huge outcrop of stone anchored here like a ship since time immemorial. The monk raises his head to glance at the serpentine Durance, constantly uncoiling its steely-grey loops down in the valley and which has lead him instinctively upstream to the confluence of the Durance and the Bléone, towards the strange, reddish-coloured procession of his fellow brothers to whom he seems to call out a greeting. These monks have been petrified in stone as a penance, in the same way as Jacob's wife who could not resist the temptation of turning back to witness the destruction of Sodom (despite the prohibition of the Almighty). They are over there, on the left bank of the river, at Mées, where Saint Donat from his refuge in the Lure prayed for the departure of the Saracens who continued to exact a high price from the land in the high valley of the Durance. His prayer was finally granted by the Baron of Bevon, the lord of Mées, who succeeded in getting rid of them and who had accepted as part of his war booty seven splendid Moorish women. They came to live in his castle. But soon the beauty and behaviour of these beauties caused a commotion in the population. Saint Donat made the Baron promise to separate himself from these daughters of perdition. However, he was not entirely confident that this would happen and entrusted to his monks the mission of checking that the Baron kept his word... To do this, he asked them to line up like vigilant sentinels all along the left bank. Unfortunately, the flesh remains weak, even when clothed in a monk's robe... When the monks caught sight of the seven Moorish women bathing in the spring water, they gave such irrefutable signs of their emotional turmoil that Saint Donat, from the heights of his hermitage, turned them into stone "in the very attitude of their desire". It is said that their penance will be over when they become totally black. For the moment, they have got to a brownish-grey, which ensures that we will be able to admire the spectacular sight for a very long time yet, a sight which was an inspiration to Gaudi, the Catalan architect who designed the *Sagrada Familia*.

Up on the rocky spur of Ganagòbi, the monk has vanished, for fear of the thunderbolts of Saint Donat... A stony plateau, a land populated by goats. Water on hillsides The spring on the plateau. Hill of light... Here we have the enigmatic etymology of this "oppidum" with its phantoms of times past, ruined churches amidst the tangle of holm oaks, scrubby bushes and blocks of stone, burial places, ramparts, menhirs of standing stones, hundreds of haystacks, of pools, of water reservoirs, springs in the rock, of balsam trees which sheltered neolithic man, hermits and then the Resistance fighters (such as at Fort de Buoux). All cultured civilisations have made their way up here, mixed up in a time scale which only a rational, Cartesian mind could unravel; they survive by offering up to us as signs the tangible and subtle marks of their mysteries. The greatest source of pleasure offered by this "île en plein ciel" (it was so named by Guy Barruol, the expert in antiquities and Romanesque Provence) is that of losing yourself then finding yourself, to lose yourself again in these geological and temporel wanderings.

Ganagòbi's history is closely linked with the history of Cluny Abbey and the local bishops and nobility and then with the history of Provence as a whole. The founding of the priory dates back to 945: it was Jean III, bishop of Sisteron, who had it built and then gifted it to Cluny, which already had immense influence. There is nothing surprising about that when you know that the spiritual patron of the Burgundian abbey at that time was no other than Saint Mayeul, who was originally of a Provencal family who had possessions in the dioceses of Sisteron, Riez and Apt. Decadence, renewal, a further fall into decadence, the history of Ganagòbi will always have its ups and downs, with a few amazing characters coming on the scene, like the Comte of Malijai and Jacques Gaffarel, Richelieu's librarian.

Today, people still come to admire the famous Romanesque gateway dating from the XII century and, in particular, the 70 square metres of the most beautiful mosaic flooring in France, designed in 1126 by Pierre Trutdert, one of the monks at Cluny, and entirely restored. It is in the Romanesque style with a red and black background and features the battle between Good and Evil, symbolised above all by the knight slaying a monster.

You must not leave Ganagòbi without taking a quick look at Saint Transit and his throne. In the XII century the relics of Saint Honorat were brought to Ganagòbi during a period of unrest. The custom arose of celebrating the transportation of these relics (the transition) and this is how the imaginary saint was born.

The Durance can also be admired from the elevated cloisters of the Bishops of Lurs, a village perched up high which became famous thanks to Maximilien Vox who made it the capital of graphic arts and because of a news item which remains engraved on the memory nearly fifty years later, "the crime of Lurs". Was Gaston Dominici, the owner of a modest farm, La Grand-Terre, between the N96 and the Durance, guilty or not guilty of the murder of the English family, the Drummonds? The mystery has not been solved. It is buried with the body of Dominici, who was pardoned by De Gaulle, in the cemetary at Forcalquier, which is one of the most beautiful in the whole of France with its rows of immaculately trimmed yew tree topiaries.

If you came to Forcalquier simply to satisfy your curiosity by visiting these graves or the erotic sculptures on the fountain in the square which were executed by a still lustful monk, you would be mistaken. You should come here to savour the essence of its history as the former capital of Haute Provence, the county town of an independent County which stretched from Avignon to Embrun, governed by the noble counts of Provence who were as powerful and respected as kings, especially after one of them, Raimond Bérenger married in 1220 the beautiful and intelligent Béatrix de Savoie who made Aix-en-Provence the foremost court in Europe. Raimond and Béatrix, like all parents, did not want their children four daughters – to be left on the shelf. They certainly were not! They quite simply married them off to four kings. So Forcalquier's destiny was linked with that of the whole of Europe and ambassadors, diplomats, merchants and troubadours frequented the court of the counts of Provence. The *Ferme des Quatre Reines* (the title of a novel written by Thyde Monier who moved in the noble circles of Mane and Forcalquier) is not far. It was in this great edifice that the four ladies are said to have lived, these ladies who did so much for the historical renown of the Count of Forcalquier and all of Provence. Marguerite was married in 1234 to Saint Louis, King of France; two years later Eléonore became the wife of Henry III of England; Sanchie was married to Richard of Cornwall, Holy Roman Emperor; and finally Béatrix married in 1246 Charles of Anjou, her brother-in-law Saint Louis' brother, King of Naples and Sicily!

Nowadays Forcalquier lives at the quiet pace of a little town which sometimes tries to recapture its past prestige. But perhaps more than its distant past, it better remembers how it became well-known in the XIXth century because of its Jesuit College – the second in France – established in 1816 by the Bishop of Digne, Monseigneur Miollis, the very one who became a character in Victor Hugo's play *Les Misérables*; famed, too, by its organisation of the "Jeux Floraux" (the floral games) in 1872 and the international festivals of Latinism in 1882, in which the erudite writer Léon de Berluc-Perussis actively participated...

Located between the Lure in the north and the far eastern point of the Luberon where you encounter the Durance at Volx, the region of Forcalquier, which does not have the same coherence as the Apt region, is perhaps one of the most attractive in Provence through its culture, its heritage and its curiosities (among them the numerous "cabanons pointus", typical country cottages) as well as its sky, the clearest in Europe. Thanks to this natural advantage it was at Saint-Michel that the National Observatory (one of the best equipped in the world) was set up at Saint-Michel. The domes gleam in the sun like interstellar flight bases and put the numerous pigeon lofts of the region (for the most part derelict) in the shade. The finest and best preserved pigeon lofts are at Limans, a little village in a dead-end on a knoll overlooking the valley of the Laye, a tributary of the Largue and dominated by a 900 metres oppidum. All square shaped they were constructed in the XVIth and XVIIth centuries, such as the one at Terre du curé Saint-Martin with its flight holes in the shape of a muff or the one at Pré du Maire Caton (15 metres high) or the ones at Fontvieille and the Ybourges valley. From high up in his "Jas du Revest Saint-Martin", Pierre Magnan can at leisure gain access to the local houses, discover family secrets and intimate love affairs, for our delectation.

A few kilometres from Forcalquier and Manosque, between Volx, Dauphin and Saint-Martin-les-Eaux, in the hills of the Pélicier national forest situated in the eastern sector of the Luberon National Park, geology allowed itself a flight of fancy by creating in its bedrock a stratum of rock salt 25 to 1000 metres thick, buried at a depth of between 300 and 1 200 metres. Because the salt is malleable and watertight, 36 cavities in the shape of bottles lying on their sides (400 metres high, 50 metres in diameter, with a narrow neck of only 45 centimetres and a unit volume of 100 000 to 500 000 cubic metres) were dug out, starting from 1968, by a company representing the big oil multinationals, in order to stock strategic reserves of French hydrocarbons. The system, whilst being very simple was no less ingenious: the hydrocarbons are transported by an underground pipeline over a distance of about 100 kilometres from Lavéra over the "étang de Berre", whilst the brine which cleaned the cavities are sent in the opposite direction by another pipeline into the pools at Lavalduc and Engrenier.

But since the end of the eighties, these strategic reserves ars no longer needed. Petrol consumption is only half what it was in 1973 and the Pélicier reservoirs are only used at about 10% of their capacity, resulting in a loss and a heavy one at that. Because high finance, like nature, hates a void, the oil companies wanted to block up the reservoirs. They decided to do this purely and simply by filling the cavities with Europe's unrecyclable industrial waste, after converting this into a necessary molten state. This was the infamous "Geofix" project which was in total contradiction of the Luberon Park Charter, and which raised a storm of protest amongst the population and the politicians who succeeded in preventing it. But for how long?... Since big business never buries a project, even if this project involves such interment in its procedure. The experts affirm that the waste disposal plan should never see the light of day. Who can know with certainty whether underground pollution might not resurface one day to affect the ground water of the Durance which is only a stone's throw away and which runs into the vast fruit-growing area of Manosque? It would be well-advised to avoid such a Trafalgar-like disaster especially since there are such negative associations at nearby Valensole, birthplace of Admiral Villeneuve who lost the battle of Trafalgar!

The hills of Manosque, much loved by Giono, climb up to Valensole. In this open countryside of the Alps of Haute Provence, you are always on a knife edge, at the hard frontier between life and death.

The death of certain villages and hamlets of this strange land, like *Un de Beaumugnes*. These villages and hamlets have returned to a natural state, where rock, vegetation and animal life mingle because, on the worst day of his life, feeling a sense of death in his soul, the last inhabitant had to abandon his home and luckless land. I am thinking of Redortiers, Monsalier-le-Vieux, Châteauneuf and other skeletons fossilised in a geological time which is on a human scale, insignificant to those who simply glance indifferently at the map but so painful to those who have to go and rebuild their lives somewhere else. Sometimes, there is a glimmer of life and hope, as at Le Baguier, near to Seillans in the Var, which, in the sixties saw the arrival of a young sailor from Toulon and his fiancee; they had decided, thanks to the "Prix de la Fondation de la Vocation", to breathe life back into this hamlet.

I have bitter memories of this period when Provence was falling into decay in the solitude of poverty, when Germans and English people lay in wait for this to happen, in order to buy up for a pittance whole villages for sale, villages whose souls were beyond price. The situation has not ended. It is insidious. How many villages are there where the elderly who can still get about have nothing else to do but to watch the funerals, speaking Provencal but with death in their eyes? How many villages have received the Last Rites, preparing for death in their fallow fields? Other villages finally died at the will of the Government as a result of the policies of regional development, such as Savines or Ubaye, or through the intervention of the Army, such as Broves au Plan de Canjuers. I travelled despairingly through the 35 000 hectares of the bare but sublime countryside like the Corniche of Verdon, which separates Verdon from Valensole, between the region of Draguignan and the Corniche of the Grand Canyon, where rocks, sheep and isolated buildings mingle in the splendid silence of the beginning of the world and where a single musical sound comes to my ears, the sound of the sheep bells carried by the strong wind. It was just before the grass of these fertile moors was devoured by the military shells. I had taken my last walk in Brovès, through places where there were as many beehives as sheep. I had spoken to Damien Cauvin, the shepherd with the biggest flock in Canjuers (1000 sheep) who had known "Mother Bousquet" who was called the "witch" or the "wise woman" from the name of the farm where she lived; she used to gather the wonderful herbs, boil or infuse them in large cauldrons and concoct her magic brews.

Rougon is not far from here. "Un de Rougon" (the one from Rougon) was the teacher Isidore Blanc, the man who initiated the exploration of the Grand Canyon, this *magnificent sabre slash* according to Clemenceau's expression. Le Tigre (the tiger) elected M.P. for the Var from 1885 to 1893, came to Roquebrussane on a visit to his friend, Victor Reymonenq, a former worker at the Toulon arsenal who was a Senator and fellow campaigner alongside Clemenceau. At the beginning of the century, Isidore Blanc dreamed of the Verdon of legend, the lair of untamed man. No-one ventured down to the canyon depths, not even the wood-cutters. At that time Aiguines had eighty woodturners! The boxwood roots snatched from the Verdon gorges arrived in their waggon loads throughout the region which specialised in the manufacture of bowls which the womenfolk studded. Then the sets of bowls appeared on the market, replacing the boxwood ones and thus robbed a whole region of its work.

One fine day, August 13th 1905, Isidore Blanc, the caver Martel and four friends ventured into the unknown. When they climbed back up to Rougon, they had the honour and the joy of having discovered this Verdon, which over a distance of 175 km from its source in the Allos Pass up to its confluence with the Durance forms the most extraordinary canyon in France. Today this self-same Verdon has become the jewel in the crown of the National Park with Castellane and Moustiers as the principal towns.

At Castellane, apart from its being the fief of a great family in the history of Provence, the festival - Le Pétardier - which is both a feast and a procession, is a reminder to the townspeople of the Huguenot siege which their ancestors had to endure in 1586. This commemoration brings into the limelight a woman who is more or less a legend, Judith Audran. It was thanks to her that the Huguenots lifted the siege. The festival takes its name from the "pétards" the heavy bronze shells filled with gunpowder which the Huguenots used against the town.

I never go to Moustiers without climbing the way of the cross to the chapel of Notre-Dame de Beauvoir (Bèu-Vezé) who was reputed to revive dead children even if they had not received baptism. The pilgrimage to the shrine continues today on September 8th; they say a dawn mass *la diano* at 4 o'clock in the morning. My own pilgrimage consists in the contemplation of the *Cadeno*, the wrought iron chain, 227 metres long which links the two great *baus*, supporting in the middle, at a height of 200 metres, a star weighing 400 kilos, 80 centimetres across; the star which protects the town.

Legend has it that it was a thanksgiving from a baron from Blacas. Having set off for the Crusades, he was taken prisoner by the Saracens at Damietta. He then swore to the Virgin of Beauvoir that he would hang the five-pointed star of the Blacas over the village if he returned safe and sound. He did come back and he kept his word. Although destroyed on several occasions the *cadeno* and its star have always been restored.

Mistral has sung of the legend in *Lis Isclo d'Or*. The first lines are inscribed on the rock face which overhangs the way of the cross:

A ti pèd Vierge Marìo
Ma cadeno penjarai
Se jamai
Tourne mai
A Moustié dans ma patrìo

(At your feet O Virgin Mary - I shall hang my chain - If ever I return - To Moustiers in my homeland.)

Moustiers is also synonymous with the porcelain which rivals that of Marseille in fame. There are only two towns which made it at the beginning of the XVIIth century. In the notes of François Carbonnel, who was a notary at Moustiers, there is to be found the act by which, on November 4th 1659, Antoine Clérissy and eight other potters signed a contract with M. de Demandol, the lord of La Palud, to have the right to extract clay from his lands. It is said that the secret was passed to the first Clérissy by a monk of Italian origin Lazarre Porri, a prior and bursar of the monastery established at Moustiers. Even if the Moustiers porcelain are only copies of the old originals and often mass produced around Toulouse, this village, founded by the monks of Lérins in the Vth century, still has the prestige of a fine legend, which has a sacred quality and is envelopped in artistic tradition. I cannot stop myself from seeing once more the 300 mules and donkeys laden with cases of porcelain being led dowm to Beaucaire to the great fair and then led back up again, even more heavily laden with Cornish tin, lead, Uzès clay and ochre from the Apt region.

The porcelain from Apt was produced in the factory at Castelet-lès-Luberon a century later, in 1728 and it made up for the lapse by its extraordinary technique. The East India company flooded the market with Chinese porcelain; Moustiers began to export to Europe, America and the West Indies. In addition, the Treasury coffers were far from overflowing (nothing new in that) and they decided to send some silver and gold plate to be melted down. To confront this new situation the potters were encouraged to create porcelain not only to compete with the Chinese but also to copy the silverware of the great families and preserve the designs for posterity. The baron of Brancas, Lieutenant general of the Army, ambassador to Spain and then Marshal of France and lord of

Castellet gave César Moulin all he needed to set up his factory on his land. Apt porcelain took off and only failed eventually as a result of English competition. In spite of this, two great porcelain makers, Léon Sagy and Joseph Bernard, continued to practise their art, the latter creating in Morocco the Royal Academy of Ceramics. Today Bernard's grandson, Jean Faucon, has inherited his grandfather's secrets and continues his tradition. The originality of the Apt and Castellet porcelain comes from its composition following different techniques, superimposing different mixes of clay which gives rise to the special qualities which characterise this porcelain: a marbled effect, jasper, "nougatine"' and "brocatelle".

If Moustiers and Castellane at the far end of the Alps of Haute Provence and the Var are the two poles of the next created Verdon National Park, this park covers in particular the Var communes of Bauduen, Baudinard, Aiguines, La Palud, Trigance, etc.

Since we have crossed the great canyon of Verdon, let us linger on the pathways of the Var. From Moustiers to… Fayence, there is only the small step represented by the association of word play (faience means porcelain in French). Enhanced all the more so as Fayence gleams in the sunlight, sending its reflections shooting across the sky. It is the sun glinting on the wings of the gliders. Behind the houses of this vast basin, there is yet more brightness, the ski slopes of Lachens and Audibergue.

I have always liked to emulate Louis Henseling, the friendly Toulon author of *Zigzagging through the Var* (the title of his numerous little pamphlets from the 1930s) zigzagging between sea and mountains, across 118 000 hectares of holm oaks and 100 year old sweet chestnut trees of the Massif des Maures, which is swallowed up by its sea of forest around the Dom, theatre for the exploits and amorous meetings between Maurin and the beautiful "Corsican" Tonia who shot him dead. Jean Aicard, another native of Toulon who lived at La Garde, had also haunted the secret pathways of the Maures at the beginning of the century, in search of characters and anecdotes. It was in the little village of Mayons that he is said to have encountered his hero in the person of a poacher named Ernest Clavel.

Today the story of Maurin des Maures no longer entertains the rare village gatherings. Maurin has been forgotten as has the Provencal Pygmalion. Yet, it was in reaction to Daudet's Tartarin who played such bad tricks on the people of Provence that Jean Aicard invented his free-thinking hero, fired by a sense of social justice and a real hunter, too!

What is really exceptional about Les Maures is that you can only see… les Maures! I can tell you this with a first-hand knowledge of the facts: I got lost there in the wilds, far from human habitation. At the ancient site of Fraxine, La Garde-Freinet, the heart of the "Massif aux Tortues", at an unassailable vantage point, the Moors launched numerous expeditions into Provence and the Languedoc in the xth century, relying on Cap Benat, where the former President of the Republic, Vincent Auriol, retired to write his memories. This location is eminently suited to all forms of retirement on the part of Presidents. Brégançon welcomes them with open arms. The massive silhouette of this Medieval fortress, whose culverines and canons always pointed to the west on the orders of Bonaparte, but which are purely decorative now, certainly provides food for both political and geographical thought, at a height of thirty metres above the sea.

Let us go back up to the Maures without Maurin but still in the company of Jean Aicard who gave credit in his writings to the legend of the Gonfaron donkey which features in the postcards of the town.

"Gonfaron is to the Var what Martigues is to the Bouches-du -Rhône", wrote Jean Aicard on the frontispiece of his book "Maurin des Maures" and he made nothing but friends in referring to Gérard de Tenque from Martigues. So it was from Gonfaron on the feast day of the curious Saint Quinis that the donkey flew, because of a whim of its owner, a miscreant of the worst kind, who refused to sweep in front of his door, as was the custom, so that the saint carried in procession could pass without being inconvenienced. *"If the saint cannot pass on foot then let him fly"* the man is reputed to have shouted angrily. The pilgrims and their saint had, however, to put up with floundering in the mud. A few days later, the recalcitrant man's donkey escaped from his stable, climbed up to the chapel where his master finally caught up with him. The one was chasing the other round and round the holy place at such a speed that they were thrown out by centrifugal force into the void surrounding them… Standing by the donkey's remains, the townspeople made the sign of the cross and said: *"The donkey has just flown, Saint Quinis has taken vengeance".* However, another less official version would have us believe that a straw had been put up the donkey's backside

and, with everyone taking turns to blow up it, the animal became inflated and took off like a hot-air balloon!

It was from Pierrefeu, near Cuers, (where the lovely Marcelle Drutel passed away in the 1960s) that the Dixmunde set off to cross the Mediterranean. Unfortunately, this Zeppelin, which the Germans had promised to France in the Treaty of Versailles, crashed into the water on December 21st 1923.

Finally, it is from Cogolin, a village of pipe-makers and weavers that the carpets woven on the biggest loom in Provence and destined for the palaces of the Aga Khan, the Trianon and the White House, as well as the ferries Normandie, Flandres, Maréchal-Lyautey, and the Liberté, started their journey.

For me, the Maures will be forever linked with the memory of Saint-Exupéry bound up in his childhood fantasy. I tracked him down in the great rooms of the Château de la Môle, hidden away in the Dom forest, between Bormes-les-Mimosas and Cogolin. When he was five, the little boy lived out enchanted days there. Tonio, as he was called by his maternal grandmother, Mme de Fonscolombe, the owner of the château, was truly the Little Prince of La Môle. The memory of Saint-Exupéry is to be found in another Massif, the Luberon, at Oppède-le-Vieux.

The Corniche of Les Maures is part of the very special window displaying the summer snapshots of the Côte d'Azur. The other seasons allow the natives of the region to rediscover a certain peace and quiet, to get together around the Bravade at St-Tropez or the one at Fréjus in honour of an old woman, Misé Berthole, to sail to the wonderful islands of Porquerolles, Levant, Port-Cros (National Park) or Embiez, whilst preparing themselves for the next onslaught of invaders.

It's in the field that I got to know the Var, as I did Provence, rather than from books. I really believe that there is not a single village that I haven't visited. In addition, when I mentally unfold the map of the departement, I am faced by a fine sense of disorder which is not always the effect of art. It is pinpointed by so many multicoloured little flags like so many milestones on my journey, each colour referring me back to a face which moved me, to a monument which had amazed me, to a location which had enchanted me or to an event which made me react, to such a degree that I don't know where to start. Hence the zigzags which I referred to earlier.

So, between the Maures and the Verdon, the little flags of Montfort-sur-Argens, Trans, Aups, and Barjols flutter gaily, stir up my curiosity through their unusual aspects, outside of time, which make up the imaginary museum of Provence.

If I were to say that boats made of reinforced concrete floated, would you believe me? At Montfort-sur-Argens this miracle took place! A plaque fixed to one of the last houses in the village commemorates its son, Joseph-Louis Lambot, who invented no less than the reinforced concrete boat. It is generally recognised that reinforced concrete was invented by Joseph Monier, a horticulturalist from Gard who set up in Paris as a specialist in rock gardens in 1863. But we tend to forget Lambot who from 1855 had obtained a 15 year patent for his work. The first boat constructed by Lambot sailed on the Miraval Lake. Two such boats decorate the peristyle of the Musée du Pays Brignolais and the Musée des Arts et Métiers in Paris. A model of the famous boat still exists at the headquarters of the Société d'Etude de Draguignan. It goes without saying that the boat did not achieve the degree of success hoped for by its inventor.

No greater success than the "air well" designed and built in 1941 by the Belgian engineer Achille Knapen who had retired to Trans. This strange work of art which was designed to automatically recover moisture in the atmosphere has a circumference of 15 metres and a height of 10 metres. Positioned like an enormous block on the little hill at Clos de l'Hermitage, it looks like a kind of gigantic anthill.

Finally at Aups, the "Factory of Abbé Jean" is a curiosity hidden in a private house in the village. The character known under the name of Abbé Jean, the incumbent of the living of the collegiate church at Aups in the middle of the XVIIIth century made no denial of the fact that he was living in the Age of Enlightenment. He devoted his whole life as a scholar and artist to a search for enlightenment and to devising an amazing synthesis of all knowledge. At the bottom of his garden, he built a curious colonnade made up of cylindrical pieces of an aqueduct which might have served to carry Vallauris water and which had been put out of service as a result of a build-up of limestone concretions. On these columns he engraved a sort of digest of all human knowledge; all the great dates of all the great names in history since man's origins, right up to the middle of the XVIIIth century are mentioned; in addition the drawings and plans of the most notable monuments. The colonnade, a veritable fountain of knowledge, is linked to a remarkable globe as well as a sundial and, more unusually, a moondial. Finally, a map engraved on the tiles of the main room of the house representing Europe, with Aups as its centre, completes this surprising "factory" (to be taken in the Provencal meaning of the word, as a place where something is done). I had the privilege of marvelling at this folly about thirty years ago; I hope that successive owners or tenants have avoided as much as possible the ravages of time on this baroque jewel of local heritage.

As you can see, Provence is not just an ecomuseum of Roman, Greek and Gallic times. The château of La Verdière is another example which can testify to this, with its 10 000 square metres of roofing, its 365 windows, its 260 rooms of which 84 are bedrooms, stuffed full of period furniture, tapestries, pictures and porcelain. It was owned by the Houses of Castellane and Vintimille, their most glorious ancestor being the Great Palamede de Forbin, the counsellor of King René and Chamberlain of Louis XI and whose political subtlety acquired Provence for the Crown in 1481 – *"not as an accessory to something more important but as an equal partner, not absorbed in one body to live together in the same way, but rather joined together inseparably but following a different way of life, appropriate to it."* Fine words which reflect the sincerity of those who signed the historic contract. It was, however, revoked in 1539 by the Edict of Villers-Cotterêts, which removed Provence from all administative and legislative acts. We must remember that in 843, the Treaty of Verdun attributed Provence and the Comtat of Venaissin to Lothaire, one of Charlemagne's three sons. The Kingdom of Provence was created in 855 for the third son of Lothaire, Charles. In 1032, Provence was attached to the Holy Roman Empire before it was split between the Counts of Barcelona and Toulouse. The "good" King René inherited it in the mid xvth century. The history of Provence is written in the royal inheritance, in the conflicts between the Lands of Empire and the Lands of Kingdom, in the plotting, the battles, the alliances and the marriages between the noble houses.

Barjols invites you to learn the Dance of the "Tripettes" when you are there as a family for the feast of Saint-Marcel on January 15th. To cut a long story short, let's say that it resembles Saint-Guy's Dance which is like the majority of so-called modern dances. All you have to do is wiggle about on your two feet, swaying when you hear the famous "air des tripettes" which from morning till night resounds like an obsessive refrain in the squares and in the bistros as well as in… the churches, where the clerics and laiety alike jig about in chorus! The basic difference between this and modern dances is that it is a traditional dance. A tradition rooted in two consecutive events: the seizure of the relics of Saint-Marcel from Montmeyan monastery by the citizens of Barjols who wanted to gain the advantage over their rivals from Aups (the monastery being almost equidistant from both towns, the exact distance had to be measured and the closest town would have the relics); the arrival of the men of Barjols in their village coincided with the women washing tripe to commemorate, according to custom, the ox they found in the village when it was under seige and which saved them from famine. Out of a sheer sense of joy, they all began to dance.

The tanneries at Barjols provided a living for the people there for many years, in the same way that bauxite mining which stains the countryside red, remained the principal industry until very recently, and plum growing the main agricultural activity. In the xvith century, the Count of Vins, who was a bit of a tyrant, so annoyed his subjects that they chopped down – or so it is said – in one night the 30 000 trees which belonged to him!

La Sainte-Baume has never held such a fascination for me as the Lure or Luberon mountains. In spite of its mystic radiance, it leaves me cold – Of course I'm exaggerating to make a pun! – like the ice houses of Font-Frège or Rougier which you would take to be modest little stone cottages. In reality, they are wells about 15 metres deep which were created in the xixth century to exploit the natural ice formed in winter in the frost basins. This ice, when cut into blocks, was thrown into the wells. In the summer, it was brought up again and taken down in carts to Nans, Auriol, Aubagne and Marseille where it was sold in the Rue de la Glace for 8,50F for 100 kilos! This is not such an old story which seems as if its taken from a real cockand-bull tale…

Like many kings and natives of Provence, I have made my pilgrimage to the Sacred Grotto beneath Saint-Pilon where the angels raised up Mary-Magdalene seven times a day, – so legend has it! – ostensibly to expose her to God's radiance and allow her to better sing his praises.

Mary-Magdalene was in the company of Mary Jacobé and Salomé, Sara Martha her sister, Sidoine, Maximin, Marcellus, and Lazarus, the brother who had been raised from the dead, on the boat which ran aground on a beach in the Camargue. Some stayed there, others went on an evangelising mission to Tarascon, Marseille, Arles, Aix; Mary-Magdalene disappeared into the countryside and was captivated by this massif extending over a distance of 12 km and 1 000 metres high. She threw herself body and soul into the solitude of the forest of oaks, cedars, maples, and sycamores, where rock masses left yawning grottos, a place fitting her penance so that she might forget forever her frivolous royal youth spent at the family villa. She stayed 33 years (the lifetime of Christ) before dying in ecstasy in the arms of Maximin. The latter had her body embalmed and buried her in the very site of the grandiose gothic basilica of St-Maximin, which was built by Charles II, Count of Provence, in the XIVth century. Since then, the Sacred Grotto of Sainte-Baume has been the object of veneration of kings and queens and still welcomes breathless pilgrims to its shrine. There is popular worship of the relics too, which, like all self-respecting relics, were stolen then rediscovered in the crypt of the basilica alongside the other Provencal saints, Maximin, Sidoine, Marcellus and Suzanne. Near Mary-Magdalene's sarcophagus, made of marble from Constantinople, which was cut in Rome and which serves as the main altar, the "head" of the saint reveals the skeleton of her face; next to it the reliquary "Noli me tangere" (do not touch me), the would-be piece of skin or bony tissue which came from the exact spot on her forehead where Jesus is said to have placed his fingers on the wonderful morning of the Resurrection. Everything in the basilica is to the glory of the saint, even its great organ which has four keyboards, forty three stops and two thousand nine hundred and sixty pipes and is world famous, having been made in 1773 by Brother Jean-Esprit Isnard, a Dominican monk from Tarascon.

At the foot of Sainte-Baume, the Sacred Grotto of the Greeks has become Gemenos, the Provencal Versailles, since Le Notre designed the park for the Comtes d'Albertas, just as he designed the present-day municipal park in Entrecasteaux.

I have to admit that I prefer Garlaban to Sainte-Baume, even if it does not have the honour of appearing in the encyclopedia. However, when its tonsured summit is hooded, I, like Mary-Magdalene, am transported by angels. You can see reflected in its quivering movements, the sea beyond La Ciotat and Cassis. And in the spectacular lightning of the storm, I think of Noah's Ark. Look! It pitches and tosses in the savage deluge, illuminated by divine light through a gap in the clouds. And suddenly, O favoured Garlaban, it crashes onto your Mount Ararat with a sound which echoes as far as Marseille. And the goats leap from the ark with all the animals and birds which have been saved from a terrible death. And I am as the wind over the rock and as hope born by the wind on the tip of the universe.

Around it, where the Etoile mountain range ends, turns the Pagnol constellation: Aubagne, his birthplace, the valley of Huveaune, Allauch, La Treille… all these landscapes and people who have provided inspiration for his tales and characters which have imprinted a certain image of Provence which Parisians have folklorised to an excessive degree.

Aubagne, the traditional home of the "santon" makers has not resisted the temptation of immortalising in clay the characters of the Pagnol myth. Are we for or against this distortion of tradition? The debate remains open. But what would Provence be without the popular little holy figures, the *santouns*? These little Christmas kings, naively fashioned in crude clay, painted in fresh, bright colours, which are brought out once a year to make the Nativity scene, were first created – even if they existed before this in glass or made of bread dough – at the time of the Consulat, modelled by the fingers of Lagnel Jean-Louis from Marseille, by Louche and by the Batailler brothers. Very quickly the figurines were imitated by other craftsmen like Antoine Simon, Joseph Boyer, Antoine Pastourel, François Garoutte… The first of the Pastorales, the only true expression of popular Provencal theatre in the Provencal language, was written by a mirror-maker, Maurel, in 1842 on the advice of Abbé Julien and performed in the Rue Nau in Marseille. These Pastorales heightened the popular craze for the santons and this in turn gave rise to the important Santon Fairs in Marseille and Aubagne in the middle of the XIXth century. These fairs continue today, often transformed "into exhibitions", which makes them into something smarter, in other towns. Nevertheless, the priest, the hunter, the "boumian", the carpenter, the fisherman and woman, the grinder, the old man, "lou conse", the shepherds, the visionary raising his arms to heaven are the epigones of the first traditional santons, the traditional figures in the family crib.

The santon is part of the notion we have of what is good and real Provencal. Like "pistou", "bouillabaisse", "pastagas", siestas amidst the song of crickets, the farandole on the bridge at Avignon accompanied by the sound of the "galoubet" and tambourine the jokes spoken in the Marseille accent of Olive and Marius (two of Pagnol's characters), the sardine which blocked the port of Marseille (a local tall Story), Tartarin and Tarascon, I cannot list them all, and some of the best customs like lighting a candle to the Virgin Mary so that the football team, Olympic de Marseille might win!

Which other region can boast of having supplied so many images, on the one hand part of folklore, dissociated from internal identity, and, on the other hand, whether we like it or not, integrated into the bric-a-brac of its culture! Pagnol has had a lot to do with this, of course, even if he never thought that these simplistic images would be taken from his masterly Comédie Humaine.

The "calisson" of Aix, in spite of its name (lozenge-shaped sweet made of almonds) does not exist to make people smile like the berlingot (boiled sweet) of Carpentras. The calisson is noble, chic, stylish like the town. Nevertheless it is a happy town, perhaps because I was happy there and I don't want to look further than the tip of my nose (I am speaking of my student days). I was too carefree to look for anything other than friendship, love and pleasure. What did it matter that Aix regales us with its 2000 years of history, which constitute the history of Provence? Of what importance to me was the Cathedral of Saint-Sauveur, "ugly and irregular" according to the harsh judgement of the President Des Brosses in 1739, with its tryptych of the Burning Bush by Nicolas Froment, official painter to King René and one of the leading lights of the Avignon School, along with Enguerrand Quarteron? Of what importance were Entremont and les Salyens which were destroyed by the Romans coming to the aid of the Greeks? What did it matter that Marius had crushed the Ambrons, the Cimbrons, and other Teutons in the plain of Pourrières, a village of which I only have a recollection of the name of its fine poet, Germain Nouveau. Of what concern was it to me that the Provencal Parliament passed its laws there for more than 250 years from 1501 to 1771?

What was important to me in Aix were the 440 metres of the Cours Mirabeau, especially its right bank, with its animated, expansive population and its cafes which I frequented more regularly than the university: the "Mondial", the haunt of the "pions" (students paid to be supervisors in schools) of which I was one, the "Royale" popular with the Corsicans, the "Deux G" the oldest cafe in France founded in 1793 and where the decor is the same as it was at the beginning of the XIXth century and where the intellectual bohemians cared little about being discovered in conflict with society's accepted bougeois mores. I only want to remember the soft green light filtering through the leaves of the huge plane trees and the rythmic murmuring of the mossy fountains inviting us to love, to laziness, to music. And the strolls along the Arc in springtime, following the example of Cézanne and Zola, or around Vauvenargues' château where he worked on his *Maximes* in 1744 and following in the footsteps of Picasso whose tomb is in the park.

Sainte-Victoire has always seemed like a mountain of the mind. Do the paintings of Cézanne who rebelled against his bourgeois origins demonstrate anything other than this? Do they reflect any other image than that of a mountain which has become transparent to us by dint of digging and distilling it to find its essence. It does not become lost in a tangle of unfathomable mystery. This large bluegrey mass slicing through the azure sky presence is indeed the mountain of pure reason.

Did I ever climb Sainte-Victoire? I do not know any more. What I do know is that I was constantly catching the trolley-bus to go backwards and forwards between Aix and Marseille!

I love everything about Marseille, with its centuries of excesses of pleasure and misery in the streets which lead to the Vieux-Port, with the sun on the tough skin of the men and on the fish revelling in the burning. In the blue eyes of Mad Marseille seated by the sea, watching the last "gabians" like the white hands of farewell, hours pass by without regret and the present moment is an eternal fire.

I have known everything about this town. I have eaten at M. Brun's this royalist who used to recite verse; he used to run the restaurant at 18, quai de Rive-Neuve and had instituted an immutable ritual: the meal would begin with the obligatory "huile d'olive gelée" (a jelly made of olive oil) from les Baux; anyone who refused to have some was sent home. I have sat in the tired old armchair at the premises of the *Cahiers du Sud* at 10, Cours d'Estienne d'Orves where Eluard, Perse, Valéry, Michaux, Supervielle, Camus, Char and others have rested their backsides and I have filled my lungs with Mediterranean humanism. I have met in the Péano bar, meeting place of the Marseille bohemians, all the painters gathered around Ambro and Ferrari. I have made my way in the Guérini entourage. I have frequented the corridors of power of Marseille politics, at the time of the municipal election campaign in 1965 between Gaston Deferre and his rivals. I have prowled along other backstage corridors, such as at the Alcazar around the ghosts of Alibert, Joseph Fabre (known as Gorlett and whose birth and death were witnessed by Pélisanne), and Mayol from Toulon with his sprig of lily-of-the-valley, whose great hit *Viens Poupoule* is still well remembered. I rediscovered the memory of Victor Gélu and Edmond Rostand. I have wandered through the little ruelles (alleys) du Panier beneath the racks of washing hung from the windows looking for the spirit of the poor man's musician, Vincent Scotto, and I have followed the procession on 15th August, the most authentically mystical festival of the ordinary Mediterranean people of Marseille, the Italians, Siciliens, Spanish, Corsicans, French Algerians, Tunisians, all mingled in the fervent celebration of Our Lady of La Major. I have bathed at Catalans. I have said poetry at the Silvain theatre. From Notre-Dame de la Garde I have contemplated the Greek Lacydon opening up onto the floating islands like white ruins. And I have embarked at La Joliette for the Algerian War, before seeing the arrival of the distraught "pieds noirs" (the French Algerians). Shall I own up to this? I even spent my wedding night in a cottage at les Goudes! I have only one regret: not to have crossed the Vieux-Port on the Transporter Bridge which was destroyed by an explosion in 1944.

I have travelled through Estaque, trying to find the places painted by Cézanne and I have drunk my fill of the sun on the "Calanques" which stretch from Callelongue and Cassis where the sirens have their haunts. One day I explored them on foot with a few friends and we got lost. And suddenly, against the white and blue background of these horizontal, vertical, diagonal lines like trembling mirages in the sea spray of Mediterranean light I saw two guides: Calendal, Mistral's hero, on the tracks of Estelle, and Ulysses, the great hero of Homer, whose humble disciple Mistral claimed to be.

There is Maillane. This is the heart of the other Provence which beats time with the rhythm of the ancient myths, the Provence of Mistral and the Rhone. A flat, sun-drenched Provence, unknown to the Gavots, these other Provencal people from the mountains of the interior. Two populations who do not mix or not very much. In former times they could create tenuous or more lasting links through reciprocal economic exchange. While the shepherds of Arles and Crau took their flocks up to the alpine pastures, the Gavots would go down to Basse Provence to work in the fields, especially during the harvest. These seasonal movements sometimes resulted in marriages and people settling down permanently, as was the case with Mistral's family who came from the Dauphiné but came to live in Maillane.

Mistral. He represents a past, present and future reference point for this land which could only be his. It is rare for there to be such an osmosis between a man and his ideas and a land. Maillane witnessed his birth in 1830 and his burial in 1914 in a tomb which he wanted to be an exact replica of the Pavilion of Queen Jeanne, this other Provencal myth with its two sculpted dogs which keep watch over the remains. It was at Maillane that Mistral welcomed the great minds of Europe who rewarded him by granting him the Nobel Prize for Literature. The literature of his "historic mother tongue" which was the vehicle of the great lyrical poetry of the XIIth century throughout Europe and which the 21 year old Frédéric Mistral committed himself to reviving and illustrating with his friends the Félibres.

No other author has written or sung so much about Provence. Provence is the inspiration of his work, his thought and his writing and he has given his all in return: his love, his charisma and his very being.

Sabe iéu uno Coumtesso
Qu'es dóu sang imperiau
En bèuta coume en autesso

Cren degun, ni liuen ni aut;
E pamens uno tristesso
De sis iue nèblo 1'uiau.

Ah! se me sabièn entèndre!
Ah! se me voulien gari'!
(La Coumtesso, Lis Isclo d'Or)

(Know a Countess - Who is of royal blood - In beauty and in nobility - She fears no-one, neither from afar nor on high - And yet a sadness - veils the brightness of her eyes - Ah! if I could be heard - Ah! if only you wanted to heal me!) Of all Mistral's poetry, the loveliest is heard in the lines of the first verse of "Mireio":

Cante uno chato de Prouvènço
Dins lis amour de sa jouvènço,
A travès de la Crau, vers la mar, dins li bla.
Umble escoulan dóu grand Oumèro,
Iéu la vole segui. Coume èro
Rèn qu'uno chato de la terro,
En foro de la Crau se n'es gaire parla.

(I sing of a Provencal girl - In the loves of her youth - Across the Crau, towards the sea, in the cornfields. - A humble disciple of the great Homer - I wish to follow her. - As it was - Only a country girl - Outside Crau, it is little spoken of.)

We find a reminder of Mistral in another high place, at Saint-Michel de Frigolet.

I didn't come to Montagnette for the sale of Frigolet but for Auguste Chabaud, the painter-poet of Graveson where he finally has his museum. This magnificent member of the Fauve School saw Montagnette in a totally different light. He painted it with all its scars surrounded by dark shadows and there is nothing amusing about it: it locks within itself the internal tragedy of nature and of man.

For me, the true-fake mountain will always remain the point of orientation for Mistral's Provence. In the north: Avignon, Durance and the great market garden of Provence extend to the Durance in the east; to the west, the Rhone which separates Tarascon and Beaucaire, goes down to Arles and creates the Camargue; to the east and south-east, the sails of the Alpilles fly the flag of the Star of the Magus and the Princes of Baux and navigate in a strange sea of stones which fell from the sky at Crau to bury the Giants, the sons of Cain, who ruled the country and tried to overthrow God.

Where the N7 crosses the N773 and comes up against the Chartreuse de Bonpas which constantly watches – and preserves itself from – the hordes of northern invaders on the royal route between Provence and the Comtat Venaissin, the old marshes were drained by the Benedictine monks of Saint-Andiol and Montmajour and in XIXth century were transformed into this vast market garden which feeds Europe. Between Cavaillon, Cabannes, and Noves (which displays its "monster" found in the Durance, devouring a human head like Chronos who ate his children) and Châteaurenard with its statue of a naked woman, a symbol of Durance sculpted, it is thought, by a pupil of Maillol and its *carreto ramado* both traditional and revolutionary, where people do not hesitate to play the International, and its market of national importance, where tons of fruit and vegetables leave each day; between Barbentane with its beautiful monuments like the Tour de l'Evêché (the tower of the Bishop's Palace) praised by Mistral, the keep which dominates the town and Rognonas which allows you to admire the confluence of the Rhone and the Durance, tradition and modernism combine in the waters of the grand canals, the streams which criss-cross the landscape and the farms where immigrant workers have replaced the Gavots; where cypresses, poplars and canes form windbreaks against the gusts of the mistral wind, where "micocoulier" trees and plane trees line the little roads with their soft sweetness.

To the west, between the Rhone and Montagnette, Boulbon has never departed from the tradition of celebrating the pagan and Christian brotherhood of wine. This is the occasion of the surrealistic procession of Saint-Marcellin on the 1st June when the priest blesses in the Provencal language the bottles of wine in the church. Lower down, Vallabrègues which appears up to its knees in river water, still ponders nostalgically on Vincent the poor basket-maker who was in love with Mireille, the proud daughter of the local farm owner. The descent of the Rhone leads us to Tarascon. In my case, it was the train which took me there in the middle of winter in 1956, as a young student given the job of master of the boarders at the college. My memory is of the station at night, deserted, icy cold with the savage, sinister mistral sweeping through it. I have tended to transfer to the town itself the despair I felt that night. In addition, it has the conceit of having engendered two monsters: la Tarasque and Tartarin. I find the first more to my liking than the boastful fop – even if it is rather bloodthirsty despite its transformation into coloured cardboard, in the same way as the agile Sainte Marthe has been transformed, the saint who captured the monster with her lasso, after tempting it from its lair in the Rhone, at the very place where King René had his favourite castle built in the xvth century.

How can I picture Tarascon without Beaucaire where one of the greatest fairs in the Middle Ages used to take place? *"Between Beaucaire and Tarascon - no sheep or ewes graze"*, goes the age-old saying. Not because la Tarasque had eaten them or because Tartarin had killed them thinking they were game, because their rivalry had swept all before it and there was no place for anything but the charging bull, the Rhone. Over its back they threw a bridge which thus links the land of Argence (a kingdom) with the land of Provence (an empire).

The Rhone flows to its maritime destiny, carrying with it the final wishes of its waters, in the same manner that it carried down at the whim of its currents the rafts bearing the coffins of great people with their everyday possessions and funeral expenses to the greatest cemetery in Christendom, Alyscamps. As I was also a student supervisor at Arles, I sometimes went and sat down on the empty sarcophagi which were of no other use than as stone benches and I meditated on man's strange destiny and watched the young people, as they entered these romantic lists, full of an appetite for life, and the young women of Arles seen every year in their best clothes, beneath their parasols, for the splendid Costume Festival. That day the woman from Arles is there to be seen, thumbing her nose at Daudet… I used to stay in a room opposite the Amphitheatre and, when I woke in the morning, two columns of light would shine into my window for me alone, supporting, or so it seemed to me, at the top of Corinthian columns, the splendid Venus of Arles offered to Louis XIV; and I would recite these unforgettable lines by Théodore Aubanel:

Siés bello, O Venus d'Arle, à faire veni fòu!
Ta tèsto èi fièro e douço, e tendramen toun còu
Se clino. Respirant li poutoun e lou rire,
Ta fresco bouco en flour de qu'èi que vai nous dire?

(You are beautiful, O Venus of Arles, enough to make man mad! - Your head is proud and sweet, and your neck tenderly - inclines. Breathing in kisses and laughter - Your fresh mouth in bloom, what is it going to tell us?)

Arles, conquered by Caesar, then Augustus, then Constantine, without changing its outward expression can be at one and the same time lyrical, sentimental, romantic, antique. Tragic.

Yes, tragic, when the sun circles the Arena in keeping with the impalpable speed of time. Then stops dead over the bloodthirsty golden sand, drinking in the last bright flash of the blood of the dying bull. And its last dark breath sweeps away the sun.

Another *bull* has sprung up. Wiping his swords, old El Rubio, who has the tortured face of a character in a Goya painting, simply said: *Bonito*. He was speaking of the *bull*.

Time is suspended with the sky. Nothing else exists in the world. Nothing beyond this *planet of bulls* with its thousands of spectators, who have come from all over Provence and Europe too tensely awaiting the most enthralling of combats – perhaps also the most inconceivable – that of a man dressed in gold brocade, arching his back like a woman, and a bull, black as the brands of hell. Whilst the cries of *Olé* rise up from the great lungs of the arena like the ebb and flow of the sea, down below on the sand of the arena, hair plastered down by sweat and fear, the shining *matador* has now knelt before the dark beast, waving his *muleta* of blood. Facing the beast which carries in the glint of its eyes the flash of death. And the *bull* watches the man, lowering its head, as if dazzled by his brilliance.

– *Ho! Ho! Toro!*

In the oppressive silence of the Arena of Arles, the rough, incisive shout goes up, right up to the sky, to the heart of a young woman with large dark eyes who is trying to meet the gaze of the *matador*. But he does not see her, lie is at grips with death.

The *bull* is still motionless. The matador smiles a fleeting arrogant smile, raising his face towards the sun god. Amidst the applause and acclamation of the crowd, the sing-song voice of an *aficionado* cascades from the tenth row:

– Los toros dan y los toros quitan, hijo!

(The bulls give and the bulls take - life - son!)

The bullfighter points his sword, rocking from heel to toe, the *muleta* low, almost trailing in the sand. The beast, trans-fixed, studies the strange provocation. And, suddenly, the flash of the blade pierces all the hearts in the Arena and especially that of the girl with the dark eyes. In the space of a single moment, man and beast are intermingled, at the forbidden frontier of life and death. A moment both sacred and profane. You can imagine Theseus in *trajes de luce*, sacrificing the Minotaur for the sake of Ariane's beautiful dark eyes.

There is always blood on the arena. Of man or beast. Inescapable. The blood of love offered up to the dying of the light once the final *Olé* has resounded.

In this Amphitheatre, the oldest after Pompei, I have been to many bullfights. I have seen Antonio Ordonez use his cape to engage the bull in an endlessly powerful *faena*. I have seen Paco Camino, the mere eighteen year old stripling, kneel in front of the bull, offering himself like Christ on the cross, pushing madness to a semblance of suicide. I have seen Ortega Puerta gored twice and yet return alone to kill his bull. I have seen Julio Aparicio, Chamaco the Intrepid; I have witnessed the crowd acclaiming the dramatic elegance of Luis-Miguel Dominguin. And I have seen the *novilleros* from Arles and others, already confirmed in their art, like Jean Triboulet, a medical doctor from Saint-Gilles, express their skill and passion for the bull.

Because here, in the Arles region, the cult of Mithras is to be found since Caesar's legions who had just conquered Marseille in 49 B.C. entered the town with their emblem of glory, the zodiacal bull.

Where the sea and the Rhone do battle, accompanied by the same wild love song, there we find the bull again. Black herds with nostrils steaming. And Solutre's horse free of all shackles. The Camargue of sun, wind, birds and strange beasts. Such as this beast of the pool of Vaccarès which the herdsman Jacques Roubaud once met and which haunted him all his life; this fantastical beast which came to take refuge at the heart of this primitive land, fleeing from earth's evolution and which sank down into the depths of the pools despite the best efforts of the herdsman. An ancient beast, both pagan god of this land and its profound soul. This *Bèsti dòu Vaccarès* of Joseph d'Arbaud will remain for all posterity as the most powerful Provencal narrative, giving a vision of this strange Camargue which the sea comes to suck at night, where sea salt gnaws painfully at man's solitude, a land where secret souls cry out like horses whinnying, stripping the vast bloodthirsty empires of rose-winged pools, unleashing the sea winds; a horse galoping till its strength wanes in the firmament of salty brilliance, up to the edge of the sea, pawing the ground amidst wild imaginings, freeing the trembling theatre of the salicorne plants reborn of love in the floating "sansouires".

When very young I learned to love this land between the two Rhones, through the medium of comic strips where the herdsmen were the heroes; and it still happens today that *The Song of a Camargue Herdsman* sung by Tino can move me more than the astonishing *astrado* of the Marquis Folco de Baroncelli-Javon…

Out of this immense mirage looms up the pale fortress of the church of the Saintes-Maries-de-la-Mer where the gypsies asemble every year to pay homage to their patron saint, Sara. The Saints hold out their hands to these ruins in their pine copse which used to be one of the most important abbeys in the Middle Ages: Montmajour.

On the other side of the Rhone, like a petrified replica of the Camargue, la Crau of the large flocks quenches its thirst at the largest pond in France; the pond at Berre which guards the memory of Georges Brenier and Hubert Giraud, two Presidents of the Chamber of Commerce, who were the pioneers of the great Provencal oil epic. Plants were set up in Lavera, La Mède, Istres, Marignane, Berre, Fos, and even at Les Martigues, birthplace of Barrès and Vincent Scotto, the marvellous musician of the "Provencal Venice", and these plants refine thousands of tons of this unseen oil. It is both the good fortune of Provence and an unsightly blot on the landscape.

In this part of Provence, caught in the triangle formed by the Rhone, the Durance and the Alpilles, the same passion for the bull takes hold of everyone. The same passion? Yes, but one that can differ in its philosophy; a difference revealed by two different names for the bull: the bull in its guise as *toro* which signifies the bullfight and the bull as *biòu* which leads to all the traditional games which this extraordinary beast has given rise to: *encierro, abrivado, bandido*, and the free chase orthe chase with rosettes. For the bull running the arena has no need of the weight of historic stone and the red of the *barrera* is often devoured by the sun and washed by the rain. The sun does not have to put on its mask of the tragic actor and smiles above the soft green of the plane trees. The sand is not impregnated with the smell of blood. Only the smell of human and animal sweat, the sweat of young men dressed in white – trouser shirt and espadrilles – and in a red "taiolle" whom you would take for dancers. But their dance is a twirl around the *biòu* and a mad dash to take the bull by surprise, to "undress" it, that is to unhook the decorations: the rosette, the two tassels and the two strings, using the four prongs of their spiked sticks. It is a game of physical prowess where death is excluded, unless by accident, which does happen: Gerbeaud, Ramos, Tosi, Toni and others have known this to their cost... It is a game where the brave bull is saluted to the gay rhythms of *Carmen* and sometimes immortalised in statue form (Cigalier, Cabrian) where the best bull-runners are celebrated like family heroes, such as Volle, Fidani, Rinaldi, Falonir, the brothers André and Roger Douleaud, Soler, San-juan, César, Pascal, Marc, Jacky!...

So, from April to October, fifty, one hundred bull-runners, for the most part novices, run in the arenas of the villages of Mistral's Provence.

It is the Provence of the bull but also of the horse whose magic hooves have the power to reawaken the earth. The *carreto ramado* hitched up to 20, 50 cart horses in single file, magnificently harnessed and launched at a great galop through the village streets send a shiver up the spine of all those who have come to watch. It is the expression of a simple but magical tradition which you have to see at least once in your life.

Do not forget that we are still on the imaginary observation point on top of Montagnette, which tries as best it can to resist the attraction of the Alpilles which it watches with a feeling of envy and admiration as they run from east to west. The Alpilles which stroke the golden fleece of the flocks against the sky. The Alpilles finding love out in the canopy of the almond trees, cypresses and eternal olive trees. And love digs out the white stones of childhood when the evening light dies in the quivering wind.

The Alpilles sweep along the souls who secretly come to take cover in the gulleys where the marvellous herbs grow, on the tracks of the summits like a puff of white angels.

Saint-Remy and the surrounding villages send their phantoms to keep watch. To watch over the rocks, trees, perfumes, over the way of life. I swear to you that I empathised with the phantom of Michel de Nostre-Dame, of Van Gogh who escaped from his asylum at Saint-Paul de Mausole, of the famous Savage, of Fortunette, the region's first beauty queen, mistress of the King of England, who held all the secrets of the healing plants brought from Brazil and who ruined herself by giving all her money to the poor; of Charloun Rieu, who came from Paradou to dance his *Mazurka souto li pin* with the others, notably with Gounod who had come to Saint-Remy to compose the music of his opera drawn from *Mirèio*. I have even empathised with the phantom of Joseph Roumanille, the influence behind the of the Félibrige whom I do not hold particularly dear to my heart.

Saint-Remy witnessed their birth and their wanderings just as it saw Glanum brought to the light of day thanks to the dog belonging to the caretaker of antiquities whose nose was good enough to snif out the first stones of the ruins. After that came to light streets dating back to the early civilisations, the Celto-Ligures, the Greeks, the Romans, fossilised but still coursing in the veins of the Provencal people. Ah! I remember with great feeling that marvellous night in Glanum when I went to the performance of *Mirèio* by Jean Deschamps! I only have to cross a fallow field covered in yellow rocket, slip through a grove of silvery olive trees to knock at the ever open door of Marie Mauron. I speak of her in the present tense since I still think of her as alive. A month before her death, I spent a wonderful day with her, full of friendship.

From her house, Saint-Remy climbs towards les Baux as if towards a cathedral of light. Indeed it is one. A cathedral of wild, white, jagged rocks above the vaste Crau. Once the coachloads of foreigners have at last left this refuge of man-gods, where Orpheus-Cocteau left the graffiti of his Testament amidst the shade and light of the quarries, then the stones can watch each other in perfect serenity and rediscover eternity, after its summer loss.

At a time when I was mad about ancient Greece, after a happy stop at Marie's house, I happened to go for a run through an olive plantation between Maussane and les Baux, beneath the folds of the Dantesque cliffs. I photographed in black and white these olives with their emaciated trunks, twisted by the earth's suffering or, perhaps, by the passion of the skies. Their great age had sculpted their form in such a strange way that it imprinted on my film, as it reflected in the mirror of my being, the allegories of certain myths familiar to me. So there was Hercules overcoming the Nemean lion, Œdipus playing out his destiny and that of all humanity before the Sphinx, Orpheus seeking Eurydice in the Underworld etc.

So I triumphantly raised my eyes to les Baux, of Balthazar, of the Grimaldi and of Prince Rainier of Monaco, streaming with light and it was if I were in Thebes, or on Mount Citheron, at Delphi where I questioned the oracle about the formidable destiny of this Greece in Provence.

Down there, at the eastern end of the Crau, Salon-de-Provence remembers Adam of Craponne, the most famous engineer in the XVIth century, who constructed the canal which bears his name and which irrigates the stony plain. But to a greater degree it remains under the influence of Nostradamus, the astrologer of kings, whose "Centuries" have never ceased to question us about their present-day or future significance, just like the splendid works of Mas-Felipe Delavouët, the great Provencal poet from Grans.

Across the Alpilles, I greet Charles Galtier at Eygalières. He is the curator of the Mistral museum at Maillane, a fine poet and dramatist and a specialist in Provencal ethnography who taught me so much. And here is Orgon, which, as it surveys the Durance from its chalk peak of Notre-Dame de Beauregard, sends it a final farewell.

I have only to step across the Durance at Cavaillon and I'm at home. I have forgotten Montagnette. It is the start of the Luberon. Already it is jutting out and I know that I am going to lose myself in its paths and forests, trying to discover the mystery of our birth at some inexistant hour to which our innate memory aspires. Once again, the grey stones of the *bòris* beckon, by the hundred between Viens, Bonnieux and Gordes, as if they had finally decided to unveil their mystery to me and then at my approach withdraw once more into their ancient silence.

Luberon, you sleepy bearer of annunciations, you will take me bodily as you must have taken the Marquis de Sade who had come to his château at Lacoste to rest and to forget for a moment his Parisian indiscretions and to learn the Provencal language by way of an erotic game with his young housekeeper; Henri Bosco who dedicated you, Luberon, to Sagittarius whilst he descended into the spiritual well of your great mystery; Albert Camus resting in the cemetary of Lourmarin. And also Clovis Hugues, the "enfant terrible" of Ménerbes, as his friend Mistral caled him, this "red" from the Midi who took part in the Marseille Commune, political orator and Provencal poet; and all the painters born here or who came for a time to search for truth in your light: Paul Guigou from Villars, Lhote and Vasarély at Gordes, de Staël at Ménerbes and Serge Fiorio, the marvellous Primitive painter from Montjustin.

Just as you must have taken bodily Antoine de Saint-Exupéry, who came back to join his wife Consuelo at Oppède-le-Vieux which he had rediscovered a few years before his death in the skies in 1944. In a final letter written to a general in 43 we have the thoughts which the Luberon inspired in him and which may seem today like a spiritual testament:

"It was undoubtedly when I was twenty that I was deceiving myself. In October 1940, back from North Africa where the 2-23 group had emigrated, my car was put away in some dusty garage because there was no fuel and so I rediscovered the horse and cart. By this mode of transport, I rediscovered the grassy roads, the sheep and the olive trees. These olives had another role than that of marking time behind the car windows at 130 km per hour. They revealed themselves in their true rhythm, that of slowly producing olives. The sheep no longer served the sole purpose of lowering the average speed. They became living things in their own right again. They produced real dung and produced real wool. And the grass also had a meaning because they grazed it. And I felt myself come alive in this one corner of the world where the very dust is scented (I am unjust, it is in Greece too). And it seemed to me that I had been an idiot all my life."

From the eagle's nest of Oppède-le-Vieux, baron Meynier, President of Aix Parliament in 1540, coveting the well-kept lands of the Vaudois, and nurturing the ambition to move in the circles of the great nobles in the kingdom, thought out the terrible "Arrêt de Mérindol", an edict condemning 19 inhabitants to be burnt at the stake and ordering the destruction of the village. Judged to be heretics by the IVth Council of

Latran in 1215, secret followers of their chosen religion, the Vaudois took refuge in the southern Alps. After terrible epidemics of the plague and other diseases which bled the country dry, they were summoned by the lords of Luberon to set up home there and work the fields under their protection. For half a century, they lived in relative peace, integrating into the local population, until the "Arrêt de Mérindol" opened the way to a veritable crusade to eradicate them from the Luberon. Soldiers of the Pope and soldiers of the King, mercenaries of the worst kind, put the Vaudois villages to the fire and sword in April 1545.

The cries of violated women, of children and old men being burned, of men sent to the galleys die away in the great silence of Sénanque. On the south side of the Monts de Vaucluse where the golden houses at Gordes cling to the mountainside, a narrow road descends into the valley of Sénancole, as wild as you could wish it to be. At the bottom of the valley of holm oaks, box trees and rocks which in summer are softened by the delicate mauve of the lavender, the light glides over the grey tiled rooves of the Abbey. Here nothing has changed since 1148, the date on which the monks of Mazan in the Vivarais, on the instructions – or so the oral tradition would have it – of Saint Bernard of Clairvaux, founded the Abbey of Sénanque, one of the three houses of the Cistercian order in Provence, the others being Silvacane at La Roque d'Anthéron and du Thoronet in the Var. Solitude, silence, light and serenity constitute the essence of a wonderful equilibrium inherent in an architecture of harmonious proportions and form, the expression of a great spirituality. It offers the message of a past time, where, according to Georges Duby, *"the organisation of the universe and the attributes of the Almighty were able to be perceived"*. Sénanque appears as the highest accomplishment of the Romanesque architectural and religious miracle.

The world stops dead in the villages on the north slopes of the Luberon which seem to have been built as so many boundary markers. Beyond is the space for adventure and the imagination, such as at Sivergues and at Buoux with the valley of the Aiguebrun, the only permanent water course in the massif, where at one time I used to come with friends to fish for crayfish at two in the morning. This was the refuge of Neolithic man, then of hermits amongst the balsam of the high cliffs, of the Vaudois, of highwaymen, and, finally, of the Resistance fighters and later of the hippies. The valley of Aiguebrun is now the rallying point of climbers from all over the world and has always been, as well as a refuge, a route for traders, salt smugglers and invading armies which had to gain control of the extraordinary Fort.

"The Fort of buoux, a ghost vessel amongst the immense, fossilised waves of the mountains, is at one and the same time, temple, fortress, humble dwelling, lofty, rock, sacred watchtower, the spirit… from which fifty centuries of man watch us." These are the terms used by the historian René Bruni to invite us to visit it.

My Provence ends in another chaos of tormented contours, of shapes and colours which I continue to seek out for their sensual beauty and in autumn for the added attraction of the mushrooms.

From Roussillon to Rustrel and Gignac, in this Provencal Colorado of ochre-coloured sand, I return to my childhood and have no compunction about covering myself in ochre like the children in Neolithic or Roman times!

The ochre comes to the surface everywhere in the cirques, cliffs valleys, fairytale rock chimneys, on the pathways, blazing in its pure white, violets, and all shades of red from Sienna orange to purple, enhanced by the acid green of the maritime pines, the softer green of the woodland pines, the violet of the heather, the white if the cistus flowers, the blue of the lupins and the yellow of the broom. The imagination can be given free rein here and attain a sense of exaltation.

Chaos, yes, but created by the open-cast extraction of this mineral by man's labours (for once man has enhanced nature rather than despoiling it) and finished off by the action of wind, rain and sun.

Legend has it that the Archangel Gabriel battled here with the fallen angels and that this portion of the earth became forever coloured by their blood. Legend joins with the poetic truth of these places, as it does everywhere in my beloved Provence.

And I am proud to believe that the creation of the world, which I glimpsed in the Ventoux, could only have taken place here in the extraordinary orgy of earth and light, the cradle of all birth and death.

Serge BEC

Preceding page:
The teeming flocks of sheep have been set free and, bleating with heightened awareness of this new life, they move off to invade the rock-strewn, life-renewing grass. Their fleecy bodies nudge gently together, tinkling with *redoun*, with *esquerlo*, with cow-bells and goat-bells which sing of the hope of high moutain peaks. The time for the rest will come with the night. The exhausted shepherds, swathed in the husky breath of the earth, will listen to the music of the angels of the night, and at their awakening, in the dew-drunk dawn, they will have the impression of having lived since the creation of the world.

Opposite:
From the extensive sheepfolds of the lands of Arles and Crau, through the alpine passes like the Col d'Allos shown here, parched by the relentless dust from the long trek, the *escabots* continue on their way towards the *amountagnage*. It's the seasonal migration. An extraordinary pastoral symphony in which are merged the bleating of the flock, the barking of dogs, the "hee-haws" of the pack mules and the calls of the shepherds who turn their gaze towards the heights of solitude and hope.

Christ in majesty giving the blessing with his right hand and holding the Holy Book in his left, surrounded by the four evangelists represented by their animal symbols: this is the remarkable twelfth century tympanum arch of the priority of Ganagobie.
On the right, the village of Moustiers-Sainte-Marie.

Savage splendor of Verdon in whose cliffs the mist huddles. The little village of Rougon *(on the left)*, perched on high, out off from the world, has held the key to this place ever since a schoolmaster dared, at the beginning of the century, to venture into its mysterious, awesome abysses, to invent the modern-day legend of the Grand Canyon and its Sublime Corniche.

Sisteron *(on the right)* opens the gate-way to Provence between its citadel and its rock of la Baume. You can descend on horseback over the rump of the Durance as far as its union with the Rhône *(on the left)*. All alone its course, through gorges and broad plaine, you can admire its steel-serpent meanderings from unspoiled viewpoints like that of the village of Lurs famous for its graphic arts and the Dominici affair.

The characters of Giono continue to haunt the endless lonely stretches of the Valensole plateau where alternating vistas of lavender and cereal crops stretch as far as the eye can see. Those from Pierre Magnan's "La Folie Forcalquier" *(on the right)*, roam forever beneath the clearest sky in Europe, the sky above this peaceful city which, from time to time, recalls its wonderful influence as the historical and cultural capital of Provence.

Magie de la Haute-Provence in its earthbound stillness traversed by sweeping skies which unite with the mountain of Lure, wild, impenetrable, indefinable. Slopes and deep valleys of pine trees, beech, larch, of strawberry and raspberry bushes, of miraculous herbs which cure all ills, the haunt of the wild boar and deer. Abounding in mystique for those who can still savour the eternal world which an aged almond tree makes blossom.

The high-point of pre-history, Vachères enjoys an exeptional panoramic view *(on the left)*. Through the Val Martine pass over Banon and through Redortiers, you ascend to Contadour. The "Real Richness" are located on this plateau from which radiate the pathways towards the great beech woods and pastoral grass-lands of the Fraches crest, towards Lure. A solitary tree gives a secret sign then reveals these vast spaces, marked forever with Giono's stamp, which provide room for the spirit and body to breathe.

With their apses shaped like stove bases, the romanesque chapels form a rosary chain across the provencal landscape and bear witness to a genuine rural faith; like the chapel of Revest in its verdant setting on the abandoned heights of Forcalquier.

Marvel at the symmetry and the autumn colourings of the fields and orchards in the surrounding countryside of Manosque and in the *plans* of the villages in the Alps of Haute-Provence, as at Banon which you can see in the distance, where the gentle mauve of the sage softens the violet of the lavender and the harshness of the terrain.

Precedent pages:
The eyes are dazzled by the magnificent colours which sing beneath the summer light, even if sunflowers and lavender are not often brought together an they are here by the miracle of photography.

Opposite:
As though forced to retreat against the cliff face by the forest, the Holy Grotto where Mary Magdalene, the repentant sinner, found refuge, has given to the massif of Sainte-Baume its mystic character. It was at Saint-Pilon, above the Grotto, that the angels raised her up spiritually seven times a day. Ever since, pilgrims have continued to flock to this site.

Ah! What a strangely subtle and unique aroma: The *rabasso*, the only word the people of Provence know to describe the truffle (the black melanosporum), which is a veritable gift from God, even if its culinary virtues conceal another which could have the power to awaken the senses… like those of the sow and the dog who know how to dig it up from the "brûlés", around the foot of oak trees.

Maurin, Jean Aicard's hero, has made the massif des Maures famous. Today, his memory is fading like the vast pine and horse-chestnut forests fade into the gray-pink mists of early morning. Mists so reminiscent of the last wisps of smoke of the ravaging forest fires of summer.

It is in hundreds of mills like the one at Flayosquet at Flayosc in the Haut-Var, that Provence converts its olives into a precious juice, without which the people of Provence would be unable to live! Each variety of olive gives a special quality to the oil.

Cotignac *(on the right)* owes its picturesque character to its cliff face, honeycombed with grottos, and its fame to the chapel of Notre-Dame-des-Grâces where pilgrims flock.

13
CRÉDIT AGRICOLE
BUREAU
OUVERT LE
Mardi matin de 9h à 11h
Jeudi matin de 9h à 11h
Samedi matin de 9h à 11h
Toutes opérations
Bancaires
Placements
Opérations de bourse
garde de titres
Prêts agricoles
et ruraux

These frontages of travel agencies or small business seem taken from an album of pictures from the pre-war ere. They speak of bygone age. And yet, the villages of Provence have managed to preserve some; like those at Rians and at Cotignac in the Haut-Var, or yet again, in the villages of Haute-Provence.

In July, lavender and "lavandin" (a hybrid of the medicinal lavender and aspic which grows lower down and has a greater yield) color the plateau of Albion and Sault with their shades of violet, mauve and blue. Beneath the crushing heat of the sun, their perfumes pour forth and fill the senses.

In the vast stony plateau of the Alps of Haute-Provence, the plantations of lavender create geometric patterns sculpted out by the dazzling light. At times, the brown of the rape seed and the yellow of the sunflowers form a splendid artist's palette. You understand why instinctive, forceful coulourists like Seyssaud and Ambrogiani painted these landscapes with all their heart and soul.

The outing by sickle of the lavender or "lavandin" is only a postcard picture for the tourist and lacking in rustic authenticity. At the end of July, from Sault where the lavender festival attracts a considerable throng to the Barronies, from the Luberon to Valensole, it's machinery that performs the cutting, bundling the plants into sheaves which will then be taken to the distillery.

The lavender fields form an integral part of the Haute-Provence landscape and endow it with an esthetic character which attracts the admiration of the tourists. These people should not forget that this beauty is the result of lengthy toil and has a very important economic purpose.

There, on the plateau of the Claparèdes, where the yellow skeleton of the road comes up against a patch of sky, rises "la borie" (in Provence, people prefer to call it *le bòri*) among lavender, thyme and broom, or amidst coppices of oak and box-wood. The *bòri* poses questions, this strange monument to the poor, and does not wish to give up its secret. In the Luberon, hundreds of these cabins, dry-built from overlapping flat stones, without binding material, bear timeless witness, simply expressed witness to a high tradition of master builders.

Lavender is often mixed in with other crops; it isn't rare to see it co-existing with cereals and orchards of fruit trees – notably cherry trees. Hundreds of distilleries (co-operative of private business enterprises) extract the essential oil from the sheaves. At the beginning of August, great clouds of smoke rise up to the plateaux, perfuming all the surrounding countryside.

Precedent pages:
The great poet René Char named it "the Eagles' mirror". And this superb image will from now on always cling to the surface of the Ventoux whose pyramid-shaped peak with its dazzling white rock-face gives the illusion of permanent snow. Another poet, Petrarch, the first to have climbed it on foot, loved "this mountain which is visible everywhere from a distance and which is almost always present before our eyes".

The frontier between Dauphiné, Provence and Comtat Venaissin, between two agricultural economies (vines, orchards and vegetables from the plain of Comtat in the south; lavender, cereal crops and sheep in the north and east), the "Giant of Provence" shelters beneath its protective spread several very picturesque villages. Crillon-le-Brave draws its pride from the destiny of Louis de Balbi de Berton whom Henri IV call "my dear Crillon" and whom he dubbed before the whole Court, "the foremost captain in the world"!

If the still, deep, unfathomable blue reigns supreme especially when the mistral has washed the sky clean, the skies of Provence, often in turmoil before and after violent storms, present grandiose sights as can be seen here above the village of Caseneuve which overlooks the valley of Apt, or in the Dentelles of Montmirail.

Roussillon suits its name well. All the facades of this village, beloved of painters, are rendered with red and yellow ochre which stand out against the snowy backcloth of the Ventoux, always within reach of one's hand but which always eludes one's grasp. The Romans had already made use of the qualities of ochre. But it was Jean-Estienne Astier who invented the ochre industry in 1785. When the models of *Elle* magazine came down from Paris one fine day in August 1957 to present the autumn collection, ochre had just opened up the tourist industry!

The first monument which strikes the eye when you climb towards the col du Pointu as you leave the Combe de Lourmarin; is the elegant bell-tower of the romanesque priory of Saint-Symphorien which springs up from the dark green mass of vegetation of the Luberon *(on the left)*. The contrast between the geology, the vegetation and the colors of Roussillon is astonisching.

The high-perched villages of the Luberon are among the most beautiful in Provence. Bonnieux with its spatial architecture in the form of a pyramid, thrusts into thc sky the spire of its lofty church, surrounded by huge black cedars. A few kilometers away, the ruins of the castle of the marquis de Sade crowns Lacoste.
The great rocky vessel of Ménerbes *(on the right)* provided a stronghold in all weathers. The outpost of the "Castellet" gave shelter to the painter Nicolas de Stael before he went to commit suicide at Antibes.

Contrary to the accepted opinion, Provence is not a land of complete repose. It must often suffer violence during the course of the seasons. When it is not being ravaged by scorching heat, or the storms which cause the rivers to overflow their banks, or the winter cold, it's the mistral that drives you mad, this cold, dry wind from the north which tears off roofs, makes the weather-vance creak on the fragile bell-towers, like the one at Pernes-les-Fontaines, and bends the ancient pines like reeds.

Autumn sets Provence ablaze with all its fires. The cherry orchards take on tawny hues, highlighted by the yellowing vines. The great forests of Lure fill with all the russets of its "fayards".

On the north slope of the Petit Luberon, the lovely ancient dwellings of Oppède-le-Vieux cling above the deep coumbs to repel the onslaught of the weather. Here, one recalls that Maynier, the president of the Provencal Parlement, launched the terrible crusade against the Vaudois.

While the storm rumbles, the fading light of the setting sun illuminates the acropolis of Gordes and its summer residences belonging to the Parisian intelligentsia. Stone reigns supreme: it has restored all the houses; all their perimeter walls and roadways which vanish into the Vaucluse, and it has built the "bories" in the shape of the hulls of capsizes ships.

Saint-Saturnin-lès-Apt *(on the left)* saw the birth of the "inventor" of truffic cultivation. Each year in February, Murs *(on the right)* offers a *Caramentran* springing up again from the tradition in which the village inhabitants take part. These two villages are typical of the Vaucluse plateau, this vast arid plinth of limestone, invaded by the sea of green oak trees, pitted with bore-holes and strewn with "aiguiers".

The provencal Colorado is the heart of red Provence. This esthetic (and touristic) chaos of rocky circuits, cliffs and fairy chimneys, is the result of open-cast mining of ochre and other natural elements. Certain birds love nesting in them or sheltering in them, like these pigeons.

The tawny flow of the cherry tree foliage enhances the beauties of autumn. The cherry is the main tree produce of the Luberon. The edible cherry is sold in the big markets and on the stalls of the traders of France; the bigarreau cherry supplies the world's largest fruit preserve factory established at Apt.

The farms situated between orchards, vines and early fruit belong to the heart of structural heritage. Rare today are farms from the Apt region which, like this one, present a tumble-down aspect but, despite all that, has lost nothing of its charm.

The blue mountain of the Luberon shelters in its shadow Lourmarin and its castle, a veritable Medici villa within Provence. Henri Bosco, in his "bastidon", wrote a large part of his work there. Albert Camus adopted Lourmarin as his own. Both have their tombs in the cemetery. Both used to love these landscapes of orchards and poppy fields.

Certain markets have crossed the frontiers and acquired an international reputation like this Saturday morning one at Apt; others take place once a year and are mainly a tourist attraction like the floating market of L'Isle-sur-Sorgue; others are essentially linked with the produce of the region and have assumed the character of a traditional fair like the limeflower market at Buis-les-Baronnies.

Certain markets have crossed the frontiers and acquired an international reputation like this Saturday morning one at Apt; others take place once a year and are mainly a tourist attraction like the floating market of L'Isle-sur-Sorgue; others are essentially linked with the produce of the region and have assumed the character of a traditional fair like the limeflower market at Buis-les-Baronnies.

Olive

The enormous rock of Saignon *(on the left)* seems ready to topple onto the town of Apt. A geological, historical panoramic landmark, it protects the site of this village perched on the northern rim of the Claparèdes.

The extensive farms of the Luberon have managed to preserve the characteristic features of the local architecture, thanks often to the intelligent way in which they have been restored.

The discovery of Sénanque with its roofs of ash-gray slates and with its pure, balanced geometric lay-out, is a rare emotional expericence for the spirit and soul. The abbeys of Silvacane, of Sénanque and Thoronet, the three "cistercian sisters", harbour such architectural jewels as the cloisters at Thoronet *(above and opposite)*.

The Ventoux watches over the "Comtat Venaissin" out of the corner of its eye, and when the broom flowers in June and perfumes the hillsides, the senses reach the height of intoxication.

In the mist-veiled light rising from the plain, the Dentelles de Montmirail are outlined like ghosts. Calcareous rocks cut in scalloped edges and embroidered with “windows”, they resemble the beautiful lace-work of some giant grandmother.

La Roque Alric thrusts its peak abruptly upwards among the Dentelles de Montmirail, like a savage cry. The south side of the Ventoux favours cultivation in "terrasses" or *bancaus, faïsses* or *restanques*… which have been an intrinsic feature of the landscape for centuries.

Like so many other villages in the arid land of Provence, Le Crestet *(on the left)* perched on its "crest" to the north of the Dentelles, seeks to slake its thirst at its fountain. A little more to the south, Le Barroux *(opposite)* lives by the clock of its castle which overlooks the plain of Carpentras and recalls the toll it used to levy for access for the north face of the Ventoux.

The old town of Vaison-la-Romaine with its pedestrianised side-streets and old-fashioned charm, looks down on the Ouvèze which flows beneath its Roman bridge and gazes admiringly at its huge open-air museum where nearly 2000 years of history intermingle, side by side. They are still counting the Gallo-Roman remains unearthed in 1907: porticos columns, sculptures and villas, such as this "house of the silver Bust". The theater dating from the first century A.D.remains the most important relic.

Grignan *(opposite)* is predominantly one of the most beautiful castles in Provence with its splendid Renaissance facade. It was in this residence that Mme de Sévigné died, and in which her daughter Mme de Grignan lived, with whom she conducted such a lengthy correspondence.
The apricot trees are one of the specialties of this provencal Drôme. When they are in flower, they tint the spring landscape with a soft white and pink light.

In this weathered landscape of the provencal Drôme where the broom flourishes joyously, the olive tree is indestructible. It is not uncommon to see some as old as Methusalah, whose twisted swollen trunks bring to mind strange monsters straight out of antique mythology. The town of Nyons and the olive tree have their destinies bound together. And let it been known once and for all that green olives are harvested green in September and black olives are harvested in December and January when the green ones are... ripe!

Capital of the Drôme Enclave in Vaucluse, Valréas is famed on two accounts: because of its cardboard packaging industry and its great fair which has now become a tradition on the "Night of petit Saint-Jean". On the 24th of June, 300 people in fancy dress process in columns up to the château de Simiane to enthrone a five-year-old child who will protect the city for a year.

"To arrive at Avignon during a beautiful autumn sunset is an admirable thing. Autumn, the setting sun, Avignon are a trio of harmonies… From a distance, this admirable town which has shared something of the destiny of Rome, bears a passing resemblance to Athens. Its city walls whose stonework is golden like the august ruins of the Peloponese, are a reflection of Grecian beauty. Like Athens, Avignon has its acropolis. The Palace of the Popes is its parthenon."

Victor Hugo
(letter of the 25th of September 1839.)

The Pont Saint-Bénézet has perhaps done more for Avignon's reputation than the Palace of the Popes. Because it's from this bridge where "dance all around" that a song went all around the world.
It was on the 21st of August 1869 that the first showing of the future *Choregies* was organized in the Theater Antique at Orange, in the presence of Mistral, which, since, has given rise to grand operas such as *La Tosca*, shown here.

The statue of Augustus salutes the crowded audience squeezed together on the tiered seats of the semi-circular theater of Orange before the fearsome and feared "Great Wall". "Sophocles still speaks here" André Chamson used to say. More recent places have been opened for summer spectaculars, like the stone quarries of Les Taillades and at Boulbon – a decentralization of the Avignon Festival – where, for example, people had the chance to applaud H.Teshigahara's *Nô*.

The Vineyards of Châteauneuf-du-Pape, the most prestigious vintage of the Côtes-du-Rhône, climb up the Rhône plain towards the keep, the imposing remains of the summer residence of the Popes of Avignon *(on the right)*.
Another stronghold on the provencal landscape, the fort at Saint-André de Villeneuve-lez-Avignon *(on the left)* with its beautiful fortified gate, reinforced by two round towers. One of the finest examples of medieval fortification.

It is the large rounded stones, once tumbled along by the Durance, that the heat of the sun is stored in the vineyards of Châteauneuf-du-Pape. The grape absorbs it by night and relishes it to produce a wine that is to be found at great tables throughout the world. On occasions, the autumn rains drench the vines which then take on that strange appearance of embroidery. You could not picture this beautiful harmonious display of dried bouquets anywhere else but at Sault, in front of a lavender-painted shop…

Among the traditional fairs, the *carreto ramado* which take place in summer between the Rhône, Durance and the Alpilles, are amongst the most popular and the most esteemed.Saint-Eloi, Saint-Jean and Saint-Roch are the patron saints. At Saint-Remy-de-Provence, the civic float with its pretty young girls, is decorated with the finest fruits and vegetables of the region. At Châteaurenard, this takes place twice: they sing the *Marseillaise* and the *Internazionale* in guise of a blessing for the "red" float of the Magdalene.

Yoked to twenty or thirty horses in line, harnessed "Saracen style", the *carreto ramado* is an acrobatic feat. The horses set at gallop through the village streets, the bridle held by the charioteers who literally fly, present an impressive spectacle to the applause of the crowd. Each village has its own particular route and obstacles. At Boulbon, it's the passage beneath the porch; at Mollégès, it's a ninety degree turn…

Ever since the XVth century, dominated by its citadel between the Rhône and Montagnette, Boulbon *(on the left)* has continued to carry out the ceremony of the Saint-Vinage or "procession of the bottles" which has its apotheosis in the great pagan and Christian brotherhood of wine. It is one of the most astonishing traditional festivals of Provence *(above)*. The Tarasque fair at Tarascon, arising from the founding of the Tarasque games and horse races by King René in 1474, has taken a more touristic direction and Tartarin is stealing a little of the limelight from Tarasque *(above)*.

Seen from the air, the arena at Arles looks like the navel of the ancient Rome of the Gauls. Blood has always flowed on the sand of this amphitheater, the blood of gladiators as well as the blood of bulls and matadors. In the Middle Ages, thanks to the influence of Saint-Trophime, the first bishop of Arles with his aura of legends, the city became one of the great centers of western Christendom. The Alyscamps bears witness to this, as does the church of Saint-Trophime whose sculpted portal is a jewel of romanesque art.

During the "Fête des Gardians", the Camargue horses rest beneath the arches of the vomitoria at the Arles amphitheater.
Place de la République, the water spout of this splendid sculpted head refreshes both man and beast.
The statue of Frédéric Mistral, place du Forum, inspired the crib-maker Jouve de Luynes.

The beautiful summer light shows at their best the costumes and headdresses of the women during the numerous traditional festivals of which the Costume Festival at the theater Antique at Arles is one. The Venuses of Arles and Provence, beloved of the poet Aubanel, reign supreme there. You only have to ask the Queen of Arles, or Magali Dunant, the gardian of Saint-Georges and all the girls in the folk-dancing groups to be convinced of it…

It was thanks to the Benedictine monks of the abbey of Montmajour, high on its hill, that the marshes between the Rhône and the Alpilles were cleared and drained. The abbey had a great influence and numerous priories depended on it.
Today, the "mistral" whistles through its majestic ruins which are still illuminated by the souls of the martyrs and the entombed warriors of the Crusades.

The beauty and the shade of the plane trees help confer on Provence an aura of opulence. Whether they encircle a stretch of water as at the château de Servannes *(see photo on preceding page)* or whether they firm a guard of honour along the highways, the plane trees are intrinsic part of the charm of the provencal countryside, just as the olive tree often planted in vast orchards in the Alpilles and which in numerous respects will remain forever the tree which symbolizes Provence.

One is tempted to say that sculpture forms part of the daily life of the people of Provence, so numerous are the examples this land has on view, whether it be at the bend of a road, on the fountains or on the facades and frontages of private hotels.
At Vallabrègues, at the time of the Basketwork Festival, the art of living is the inspiration for these light-colored baskets, so skillfully woven by the Vallabrègues basket-weavers, or whom, in the eyes of posterity, Vincent, Mireille's sweetheart, remains the most famous.

Van Gogh's sunflowers have left Arles for Aix-en-Provence and have elected to take up residence at the foot of Sainte-Victoire to make the gray shades of the mountain sing. What does Cezanne think about this?
The notion of "magic place" dear to the town planner Roland Castro, proves itself on all the market places of Provence. The one at the Place des Prêcheurs in Aix-en-Provence is a fine example of it with its stalls full of color and aroma.

A game of "pétanque", has (always) given pleasure, ever since Ernest Pitiot invented it at Cassis round about 1910, making it a rule that the feet should be kept *tanques*, that's to say, still. "Pétanque" is always at the heart of provencal comedy theater as in the game of cards immortalized by Pagnol. The "miniature provencal Village of Grignan" and the "Petite Provence du Paradou" recreate these essential elements of the provencal' *ieme.*

It is hard to imagine a chatter-free day in Provence. These young girls in the *La Capouliero* folk group in period dress, babble on perhaps about their flirtations beneath the archer of the Saint-Sauveur cloister. Pierre Graille, the crib-maker of Grambois, has even managed to make us hear the exchange of gossip between these two ladies.

Sainte-Victoire is the mountain of the spirit. This enormous blade of a mountain, snowy-white gray, blue or rose-tinted, carves into the blueness and the setting sun. Cézanne spent his life-time painting its very essence.
At its feet, the château de Vauvenargues *(above)* tells of another genius of painting: Picasso lived there and is buried there.

15

Following pages:
Between Marseille and Cassis, the white-faced cliffs and inlets hold back the turquoise and emerald waters of the Mediterranean, which penetrate inaccessible caverns painted by ancient man. When the mistral blows upon these weather-worn rocks, the voices of heroes can be heard who, from Ulysses to Calendal, still haunt these places.

Aix is never without a harmonious serenity which has its origin in the light of the plane trees of the Cours Mirabeau, in its fountains and in its squares.
The one at Albertas *(on the left)* invites you into the Music Festival. The "fronton" at the ancient Corn Exchange pays an allegorical homage to the confluence of the Durance and the Rhône *(below)*. The dome of the baptistery of the Saint-Sauveur cathedral allows the light of heaven to filter through *(above)*.

Marseille the Beloved! Ladydon de Gyptis salty embrace upon the centuries! Who would not be swept along in the human tide down the Canebière to be overwhelmed with joy on the forest of masts of the Old Port? Who would not climb the Bonne Mère to take in the matchless vista, then to sweep down to the Town Hall and meander through the back streets of the Panier on every August 15th, a rapturous crowd acclaims Notre-Dame de la Major during a mystical, multi-ethnic procession…

The three districts of l'Ile, Jonquières and Ferrières, united in 1581, founded the Martigues republic which therefore, some two hundred years before the French nation, marched beneath the red white and blue flag, the three colors of these districts. On the pond of Berre, Martigues sole resemblance to Venice is its canals which reflect the warm, polished frontages of the fishermen's houses.

The land of ancient myths, such is this spellbinding land of the Camargue, with its horses, bulls and pink flamingos. A landscape that has become well-known, the rice fields, flooded in spingtime, are experiencing hard-to-resolve disputes over its salt beds, its stock-breeding, its tourist industry and the protection of its flora and fauna. The Crau is not far away, and great *jasso* (sheep ranches), like the one at La Favouillane, give shelter to teeming flocks.

The Saintes-Maries-de-la-Mer every 24th-25th May, lives to the frenetic rhythm of guitars and gypsy flamenco. They come in their thousands from France and Europe to pay homage to their patron "Sara la noire" the servant girl of the saints Marie-Jacobé and Marie-Salomé. The "gardians" lead this fantastic procession from the fortified church down to the sea where Sara is blessed.

Inseparable from the *biòu*, the Camargue horse, small in stature, sturdy and with its white or light-gray coat, is the indispensable mount of the "gardians". As a foal, he is still chestnut or gray, and will only turn white at his first change of coat. Later, he will, like his dam and sire, gallop proudly in the "sansouire", around the pond of Vaccarès.

At Lambesc, these mechanical figures which strike the hours, are a rare little wonder. They could have been modeled on this shepherd from the *Riban Esteven* of Saint-Etienne-du-Grès and the fresh-faced and delightful twin lady musicians you find at the Olive Fair at Mouriès.

The famous Alphonse Daudet mill on the pine-clad hillside at Fontvieille takes the full brunt of the mistral as well as thousands of tourists. Despite its sails being stilled, it continues without flagging, to mill the seed of poetry and legend.
Near Eyguières, towards the plains, the provencal farmhouse disappear into the cool of the tall trees, and together with their crops, remain protected from the mistral by long lines of cypress trees.

This golden flood, swollen with merging streams of sheep, this endless countless flock, flows around the town of Saint-Remy-de-Provence every Monday at Pentecost. The gathering for the departure on foot of the summer pasture migration, from Provence to the alpine grazing lands, gave rise to this festival which the shepherds love to include in the provencal tradition.
Another strong tradition in Basse-Provence: the sport of bull running, one of which is the *abrivado* or the setting free of bulls into the town.

Jardins Van Gogh
Tectona
BOISERIES
et décorations
Ledroit
BEAUTE
CANINE
ICI

The mythical Golden Goat evoked by Paul Arène, could it not be this splendid goat to which the tiny village of Rove, near Marseille, gave its name? With its tawny coat and lyre-shaped horns, it greatly resembles it in the sunlight. It can survive in these deserted, rocky places as here in the Alpilles.

Life in the village of the Alpilles unfolds according to the rhythms of work and the sequence of days, with their simple pleasures such as this game of petanque at Fontvieille. While the flock keeps the shepherd busy, the olive harvest remains a time of great effort. The harvesting can still be done by hand, but more modern methods have replaced the old ways, notably with the use of plastic nets spread on the ground, and the employment of brooms.

Seen from above, les Baux suggest the unusual sight of a huge ship of white rock creaming a course between jagged reefs. However, les Baux continue being resplendent, and tourists of all nationalities scale the concentric circles of the Val d'Enfer, in both summer and winter, to take part in one of the most beautiful midnight masses.

Perched on their rocks pitted with dragons' caves, Les Baux look more like a sorcerer's den than the capital of the famous princes of Balthazar's star of sixteen rays of light. The present-day, descendants are the Grimaldi, princes of Monaco.

In these Alpilles, which bear easy comparison with biblical hills, and a short distance from Eygalières, the Saint-Sixte rises up to God on its gentle hill, surrounded by candle-like cypresses, which the wind causes to crackle in black flame. Towards the plain, farmhouses, often restored with ochre rendering, withdraw into their lush, sunny isolation.

Curled around the interior of her boulevards, Saint-Remy-de-Provence, dreams of the cities that preceded her; roman, greek, ligurion and perhaps of "the nameless one before history began", as Marie Mauron once said, she who lived within hailing distance of the Antiques, (in this case the mausoleum erected in honour of Julius Cesar) and the astonishing "Glanum" with its handsome relics such as this pre-roman sculpture on show at the museum.

A

B

C

I

J

The *santoun*, this "saintlet" of Judeo-Christian tradition, is one of the most powerful symbols of Provence. A doll-like figurine of the type of figures in the nativity crib, it has overcome his titles of nobility since being created at the end of the XVIIIth century. Numerous makers of these "santons", carry on the tradition of crib figures mouled in sun-baked clay, or oven-baked and hand-painted, either in gouache or tempera: still others prefer to produce clothed "santons".

D

E

F

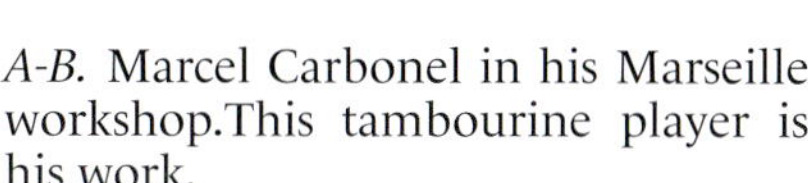

A-B. Marcel Carbonel in his Marseille workshop.This tambourine player is his work.
C. The "Coup de mistral" by Fouque of Aix-en-Provence.
D. A unique work from Pesante: "the old woman".
E. "The Prophet Isaiah" by C. and J. Devouassoux at Puyvert.
*F-G.*The "farandole" and a fine equine bust from Liliane Guiomar from Château-Arnoux.
H. "The seat restorer" by Lise Berger.
I. "The garlic selle", a unique work from Ascia.
J. "The old woman with firewood" by Mamie Martin of Aups.

G

H

Printing: may 2009
by Grafiche Zanini printers Bologna (Italy)
2nd edition